Remembering Genevieve

Georgann Lemaire

Remembering Genevieve

ISBN 978-0-9969055-0-3

The cities Genevieve lived in,
and the length of time she lived there -

This is a story of the childhood of three sisters, the Henry girls, where they came from and how life treated them.
They are gone now.
They did not become famous, you wouldn't have heard of them, I'm pretty sure.
It is told from the eldest sister's perspective.

Her family called her Genevieve, though she changed her name as a teen to one she felt suited her better.
We'll begin at the sad ending of Genevieve's memoir and then to what I imagine were her musings eleven years later when she began writing her stories.

And then she will begin her story in her own words as she is *Remembering Genevieve.*

The stories are hers, verbatim, in her order, according to the cities the family resided in. Spellings and grammar are hers.

Meiners' Oaks in 1935 was so thick with trees that most of the time, in much of the town, the sky was barely seen.

But why, why, couldn't it have been a sunny day? Their purpose at the cemetery was so dismal, so final.

The preacher arrived and took his place graveside.

> "Lewis Cleveland Henry was born in the town of Ellijay, North Carolina, on November 5, 1886, to John Thomas Henry and Virginia Moses. He was married to Eliza Jane Peek, who has preceded him in death. We commit his body to the ground, ashes to ashes, dust to dust."

The girls stood in their places, in their daze not dismayed by their second-hand dresses and worn shoes, in their grief not aware of the slivers of light sneaking down from the sky and shining through the branches on them.

Now daddy was gone, too... gone from them....

The service was short.
The coffin was lowered.

The girls turned away.

Genevieve, 17, had requested that the cause of Daddy's death not be published in the obituary notice. She had also declined to have their names printed in the newspaper as his next of kin.
The humiliation of his illness and death was more than she could bear.

Mrs. Humphrey stood some distance away out of respect, waiting to take the girls to their foster home. Grace, 12, and Virginia, 15, followed Genevieve to the car for the short one mile drive.

Eleven years later, that vivid memory of Daddy's funeral plays over and over, bringing to mind the grimness of our black and white childhood. It's where I'm cemented as an adult, though now I live in a thriving city, have provocative friends and my sisters nearby.

*Don't give me advice, don't even sympathize. Please, just be still and listen...
I already know I'm carrying a load of grief and a bucket of bitterness.*

I just need to talk about it to myself, sort it out.

It's March 26, 1946. I'm 28 years old. In writing my memories, I am trying to free myself from the underlying homesickness I feel for the Smokey Mountains of North Carolina. Would returning to the Appalachians placate my longings, pour into the hollowness I feel, fill up my destitution?

It seems that the answers to my questions about life might come from a review of the past.

I am remembering Daddy and Momma, Lewis and Eliza Henry, and how hard they worked in the fields. I recall noticing that the time came that Momma had to rest a lot, and Daddy went out alone. How Daddy must have agonized in making the decision to move away from family, farm, and livelihood clear across the country. Momma's health was failing fast and he was advised to exchange the cold, wet winters for the year-round mild climate and sunny days of California.

I am remembering my little sisters, Virginia and Grace, running free in Ellijay, and the five day train ride that brought us out west. I'm feeling thankful that we girls have stayed so close through it all.

And I am remembering me, called Genevieve by my family and friends in my childhood. How serious and analytical I was, and still am. I'm remembering how many different houses we lived in during those years, the neighbors who were kind to us, and our Momma as she began to falter in her health.

One of the first memories I can recall is experiencing the booming rumble of an airplane when I was about four years old. I was in the yard with my sister...

Ellijay

Ellijay, North Carolina
-from my birth on December 8, 1917-
January 6, 1927

I had heard some talk of aeroplanes…an aeroplane was a contraption that flew about up in the sky. I had been curious as to the size of such a thing, and had been told it was 'about as big as the house.' One day, when Momma and Daddy were working up in the New Grounds, I was playing with Virginia out in the yard, on the south side of the house. Suddenly I was aware of a roaring noise; it grew louder and more ominous and I looked upward to see an aeroplane for the first time. It looked so monstrous and made such a deafening noise that I was momentarily paralyzed. When I regained control of myself, I started screaming at Virginia and we ran, as fast as our legs could carry us, into the house…where we stayed until Momma and Daddy came back to the house to have dinner (the noon-day meal). There hadn't been any doubt in my mind that the aeorplane was going to fall on us.

One morning I awoke and got out of bed and began pondering about the way sleep had stolen upon me the previous night while I was lying in bed. I followed Momma about the house, trying to find out how 'sleep' operated. Evidently her answers to my questions, "Where do I go when I go to sleep?" and "Why don't I know when I'm asleep?" weren't satisfactory. I wondered about the demarcation line between consciousness and unconsciousness. Trying to make her understand what I was talking about, I explained, "I'm lying there, and I'm me," I paused to find words, "…and then there isn't any more Genevieve, but I don't know it."

Although the scene probably occurred countless times, I recollect just once (and the memory is dear) when Momma sat in a squeaking rocking chair, holding me in her arms, lulling me to sleep, singing,

> Low, low, breathe and blow, wind of the western sea.
> Over the rolling water go;
> Come from the dying moon and blow, while my little one, my pretty one sleeps.
> Rest, rest, on her Mother's breast;
> Father will come to thee soon.
> Father will come to his babe in the nest;
> Silvery sails all out of the west,
>> blow him again to me… while my little one, while my pretty one sleeps.

I heard the entire song and some humming before I fell asleep. It was late twilight and time for Daddy to come in from the fields to supper. And the fire was crackling.

Momma recited poetry, and I remember four lines which impressed me because of their rhythm, but which I couldn't understand:

> Backward, turn backward,
> Oh time in thy flight,
> And make me a child again
> Just for tonight.

When I was big enough to wield a broom, I liked to sprinkle the plank floor in order to settle the dust, and do the sweeping downstairs. I was extremely thorough and would become vexed to the point of tears when I found that I couldn't get around and behind the wood stove with the broom. I cried for Momma to move the stove, and she would point out that it couldn't be moved because there was a stove pipe involved. Having an obstacle like that to thwart my attempt at thoroughness somehow took a lot of pleasure out of sweeping.

The wind was wild that night. It struck the sides of the house with terrific force, and it gathered under the eaves and threatened to lift the roof off the house, just as one would lift the lid from a saucepan. The little two-story structure was straining every timber to withstand the onslaught when we all went to bed. The struggle didn't keep Virginia and me awake, so I don't know how long it was before Daddy and Momma came upstairs with a kerosene lamp, rolled us up in our quilts, and carried us downstairs. By then the house was quaking; then it quieted down for a moment. Another convulsion, and then it rocked and rolled like a ship on the sea. Virginia and I were carried out into the yard, and the four of us lay on our stomachs, flat on the ground.
We were waiting for the wind, which had assumed cyclonic proportions, to toss our home over and roll it down the hill. I don't know how long we lay there, clutching at the earth, before it was deemed safe to re-enter the house. The following morning, several chickens were wandering around aimlessly. In this case, the coop had flown the chickens.

There was only one instance, to my recollection, when I was reprimanded physically by Momma. She was sitting in the back yard, peeling peaches preparatory to canning them, and I was continually putting my hand into the big dishpan that was in her lap to pick out a slice or two of the yellow juicy peach. After warning me a sufficient number of times to keep my hand away from where she was using the paring knife, Momma had to resort to slapping my hand quite sharply.

There was a young man named Leonard who came to Grandma's house while we were all staying there and Momma was sleeping in the screened-house. It seemed that he was considered a little 'off.' He used to sing a song about the sinking of the Titanic that went thus:

> Wasn't it sad, wasn't it sad,
> Wasn't it sad when that great ship went down?
>
> There were husbands and their wives,
> And their children lost their lives.
> Wasn't it sad when that great ship went down?

He was rather tall, and as he stood near the doorway singing that song, I was entranced.

There was a period, one bitter winter, when I had no shoes to wear to school. From our house I traversed the path between the cornfield and the potato patch, past the site of the old saw mill, and up the hill to school, walking gingerly over the ice….or slushing through the snow…with rags bound around my feet.

When I had shoes, they were the high-top variety, lacing almost up to my knees. I liked them. I was constantly aware that I had shoes on. As the soles began to wear thin and holes appeared, they were reinforced with pasteboard. After having gone barefoot all summer, I could hardly wait to get into my shoes. And in turn, after wearing shoes all fall and winter, spring seemed always to be interminably distant in the future. I would ask Momma daily, how long it would be until Easter; by Easter, it was usually warm enough that she would allow me to take off my shoes for several months.

The first shoes I owned, aside from the high-top ones, was a pair of black patent leather slippers that was the pride of my childhood. I walked in them always with such care, avoiding rocks and manure piles, so that they were in fairly good condition when I had outgrown them. The proud occasion for which I got the shoes was a Mothers' Day program at the church. I also had a brand new yellow organdy dress with a sash that tied in a gigantic bow in the back. I stood on the platform in front of the pulpit among two rows of other children, and we sang a song honoring our mothers. When we arrived back home, I removed my precious slippers with the one little strap that went across the instep and buttoned on the side, rubbed them industriously with a caster-oil-soaked cloth and put them back into the shoebox until the next occasion when I would wear them.

I was walking up the path from the privy behind Grandma's house, paying little attention to where I set my bare feet. At one careless step, I felt a sharp, familiar sting on the sole of my left foot. I had walked on a bee that had strayed from Grandma's hives, and for my heedlessness he stung me properly before the arch of my food crushed him. I hobbled on to the house where someone removed the stinger. With inexpressible dismay, I watched my foot swell. That meant that I wouldn't be able to get into my shoe and the next day was going to be an occasion for which I needed them…a funeral. I cannot remember whose funeral it was, but after hoping until the last minute that the swelling would go down enough to permit me to wear my shoes, I had to go barefooted.

When I think of Bertha Moore's funeral, I always see her standing beside her own coffin, with her dark hair piled high on her head, wearing a rose on her right shoulder. Her eyes are lowered as she reads from a book lying open in her hands. She stands there while the congregation files past her casket for one last look at her body. It's as if she were reading her own obituary before being interred. That scene takes place up in the front of the Baptist Church. This anomaly is due to the fact that I combine, in my memory of her, a photograph of her in the above-described position (which belonged to Momma) and her funeral services.

I believe it was autumn. Virginia and I were entertaining ourselves by standing at the top of the bank which formed the boundary of our front yard and rolling our respective pumpkins down the incline. They would tumble down the side of the bank, across the yard, and hit the base of the house. It was a contest, with each roll, to see whose pumpkin would reach the house first. After one send-off, our two pumpkins bumped into each other on the way down the slope, and the impact sent them off their courses. I clambered down the bank and went to retrieve my pumpkin (punkin). I picked it up and turned around, facing Virginia, who was still standing at the top of the bank. She had picked up a rock and, accusing me of making my pumpkin bump hers on purpose, she threw the rock at me. It hit me squarely between the eyes and I went down under the impact. I picked myself up and, wheeling dizzily, I started across the yard, calling Momma. She came hurrying up the path from where her clotheslines were (I don't know whether she was already on her way up before I screamed, or whether she just got up in a hurry after she heard me; anyway, she was beside me before I got very far in her direction) and I held on to her to steady myself while I sobbingly told her why Virginia had hit me with a rock. Virginia was still standing in the same place at the top of the bank…and there the picture fades. (P.S. I bear a memento of the occurrence in the form of an indentation between my eyebrows, nearer the right one.)

Daddy was cutting down a small tree that grew, in a slanting direction, at the top of a bank near the house…the bank on one side of the path that led past the clothes lines to the branch where we kept our milk and butter cooled, and on to the spring where we got our drinking water. He was in a precarious position working on the tree, and suddenly slipped down the incline of the bank. In sliding, his right armpit was slashed by a part of the tree that caught him on the way down. It was thought remarkable that even though his armpit was gashed, his shirt was barely torn at all. Momma cleaned the injury, tied a clean cloth over it, and it seems as if the doctor was called to treat it.

I used to come into a new supply of paper dolls twice a year, with the arrival of the spring-summer and fall-winter editions of the catalogues. The prettiest models, I cut out and used as dolls. I cut the heads, arms, and legs off of the other models and used their clothing for my dolls, being careful to leave little tabs projecting from certain points of clothing so that I could bend them back and make them stay on my dolls. I made upright beds out of cardboard for the dolls to sleep in. Each catalogue contained several pages of beautiful samples of wallpaper. From these pages, I cut heart-shapes and fashioned them into lovely Valentines every year.

I had my paper dolls all spread out on the floor downstairs. All at once, a big gust of wind came in at the door or the window, blowing my dolls around. I got them all together and back in line and the wind began blowing in again. At that point, I was out of patience with it and started crying for Momma to "make it quit blowing!" I expected her to do just that. I was leaning frontward, covering as many dolls as I could with my arms to keep them from blowing about, waiting for Momma to turn off the wind, when she explained that she didn't control the wind and that I'd have to close the door to keep it out.

Our privy wasn't enclosed. It was merely a little table on four legs with a hole cut in the top. Beneath the hole was always a pile of excrement with flies swarming all over it…the big horse variety with blue wings. This affair stood beside the trunk of a large tree. Anybody sitting on it could be seen from the house, which made no difference, but one could also be seen from the rear by anyone who happened to be walking along the road some distance off. I remember the first time I felt embarrassed by being seen by an outsider. I hadn't yet sat down, but I was facing the seat with my dress pulled up and my bloomers pulled down. I chanced to look up and I saw a man walking along the road, so far away that I couldn't recognize him. I hastily dropped my dress and moved behind the tree where he couldn't see me…if indeed he had been looking. Perhaps the reason I had never had an occasion to be thusly embarrassed before was that I usually looked up the road to see if there were any passersby before starting such an operation.

Our backyard was dangerous to walk across. All dishwater, bathwater, and chamber contents were dumped there from the back door. This caused it to be slippery, the bare earth as well as the little patches of slimy green fine moss that were nurtured there.

There was a variety of cedar tree that grew at the outside edge of the backyard. It bore blue-gray berries at a certain time of the year and the birds swarmed around to eat them. Black birds, I think.

We knew in advance that there was going to be an eclipse of the sun, but since I'd never experienced the sight of such a thing, it didn't mean much to me. However, in the middle of a bright sunny day, when it gradually began to grow dimmer, I was alarmed. It wasn't long before the sun was in a total eclipse, and I was frightened to distraction. I was crying and clinging to Momma's skirt as she was trying to convince me that I wasn't going to be harmed. Then, as she went about the kitchen with a lamp, I huddled on the floor next to a chair. I believe Virginia joined me and we wailed together. I felt a strong and fearful conviction that the end of the world was at hand and Satan was coming out of the darkness to claim us.

One morning Virginia and I came downstairs and Momma was still in bed. As we reached the foot of the stairs, she said, "Come in and see what I have in bed with me." When she pulled back the quilts and showed us the red and wrinkled little thing that was Grace, we were somewhat taken aback with surprise…rather, entirely taken aback. But after a couple of days, Grace either improved in appearance or we became used to her as she was, and we were trying every angle to persuade Momma to give Grace to us, or to let us have her to play with at least. We came to Momma's bedside with all our 'purties' collected in match boxes and wanted to trade them for Grace. Even if we couldn't have her 'for ours' we wanted to 'claim' her.

Daddy was hovering about the bed that first morning, and it was he who cooked our breakfast, I believe.

We had a morbid curiosity in watching Daddy kill a chicken now and then by wringing its neck. We stood well aside so that when he finished the job and dropped the chicken it wouldn't flop too close to us. We watched its grotesque maneuvers until it was completely still.

Once I watched Daddy put an end to a hog. With the butt end of the axe, he hit the hog a mighty blow on the head. The dull thud seemed to resound through the air. After the hog was stunned in that way, I think someone was at hand with a gun to shoot it. This took place right in the pig pen, when the poor hog was walking unsuspectingly toward the trough where I used to dump the slop. After butchering, I was given the bladder. I entertained myself for some time by blowing it up like a balloon. For some time, we had cracklins, which I think were pieces of crisply-fried hog's skin, minus the bristles. They curled up on the edges in the frying process and then resembled potato chips.

Our cow had a calf, and it was mine to claim. I can't remember whether it was this calf or some cow that we had that died of eating some greenery (possibly poison laurel) on our land, below the path that led to the spring.

I used to spend a great deal of time sledding, during whatever season it is that the ground is covered with dry pine needles. There was a rope with one end attached to the front of each runner of a sled. Holding onto the rope, I could give myself a good send off, go scooting down the hill below our house, weaving in and out among the pine trees. After some practice I was impressed enough by my skill to walk into the house and announce that I could "guide it so good" that I could go anyway I wanted to—by leaning to one side or the other, and miss all the trees!

One day Virginia and I rode with Daddy on a big horse-drawn sled over the rough dirt road up to the Whitcomb Place. It was, I believe, deserted, and Daddy was doing some plowing on the land. As he was plowing one of the rows, he turned up a nest of brand new little baby field mice. Virginia and I spent some time with them...looking, wondering, questioning Daddy. And we were impressed with the great size of the nearby barn when we investigated it.

There is a memory of walking along the same dirt road, one pitch-black night, with Daddy. He carried a lantern and I stayed close beside him. He made some mention of wild cats or bob cats lurking in the dense trees beside the road, and I think I learned that they were afraid of light. The lantern was a consolation. We were walking toward the mill where we had our grain ground, but I don't know what the purpose of the trip was.

Out of a box of cracker-jacks came one of the prizes of my childhood…a little ring with a ruby-red stone in it. I wore it and cherished it until I lost it one day while playing in the woods below the house. I raked the pine needles on the ground in that spot for several days before I gave up the search for the ring.

Daddy was working on the wooded hillside across the creek; I think he was splitting shingles. It was cold enough so that when I was sent to carry something to him from the house, I was bundled up in my coat and mittens. He met me on the opposite side of the creek and stood there, watching me cross the fallen tree that served as a bridge. Before I left him to return to the house, he gave me a key to his trunk which he had in his pocket. He was probably afraid he might lose it while working. We put the key inside my right mitten so that I'd get back to the house safely with it. Then he stood and watched me cross back over the log. When he came home that evening, he asked where the key was, and that was the first time I had thought of it since putting it inside my mitten. It was nowhere to be found, so it was assumed that it fell out of my hand into the creek when I was balancing myself to cross the log. Daddy had a second key to the trunk but it was locked up inside it. I believe he had somebody pry the lock open shortly thereafter. I can see Daddy squatting beside the trunk, fooling with the lock.

On one occasion, I was at the mill with Wallace, Momma's brother. I think we were waiting for the miller to finish with a sack of grain we had brought him. We sat on the bridge that crossed the mill stream and dangled our legs over the side. We would look down into the eddying stream until we'd become dizzy. At that point, it felt as if the whirlpools were magnets that would draw us down from our seat on the edge of the bridge, and we'd look away to escape it.

One time, when I was upstairs working on Valentines (using a mixture of flour and water for paste), Ruby (Ammons was her last name, I think) was looking at what I had done. Grace was in the room and when Ruby saw her, she smiled down at her and said in a grown-up manner, "God bless her little heart." Instantly, I was taken aback that she had used God's name, but then I realized that she was only saying what adults said, so it should be all right. I was rather surprised to discover that she was grown up to the extent that she could mimic the grown-ups.

We attended Higdonville School while we were staying at Grandma's. There were two little girls named Mavis and Christine. It seemed that they were leaders among other girls their age. They appeared to be self-confident and were well-dressed and pretty. Mavis had bright auburn hair and I think Christine's was on the blond side. During one recess, about five of us, including them, were standing in a group and looking at a doll that Mavis had brought to school. It was like nothing I had ever seen, a celluloid kewpie doll about four inches long. She let me hold it to feel how light it was. I wondered what was inside of it; was it solid or hollow? I squeezed it between my fingers and it yielded to the pressure…I had crushed it, and I was mortified.

That afternoon, when school was out, I was walking along the road and Mavis, with a couple of her friends, was walking slightly behind me and making remarks about my having broken her doll. I was afraid of her. Two boys (I believe they were brothers and one's name was Oliver) were walking in front of me. They turned around and started taking my side, telling Mavis that I hadn't broken her doll on purpose. I drew closer to them, especially Oliver, glad to have their protection. The boys were a little older than I was, and I don't know why they took up for me; it seemed as if they may have been Moses' boys and remotely related to me. A short while, maybe a few days, later, after Oliver had been so kind to me, I sat at my desk in class and turned around and screwed up my face and stuck out my tongue at him several times. He was sitting a couple of desks behind me, not provoking me at all. He didn't even retaliate in any way. As far as I know, I was sticking out my tongue at him merely because I thought he was funny lookin' –but I hadn't worried about his being funny lookin' when he had befriended me. For a long time after that, even three or four years, I suffered an agonizing conscience when I remembered how ungrateful I had been to him. I was so conscience-stricken, in fact, that I cried about it once or twice.

Grandpa Peek had suffered a stroke. He lay on a pallet on the floor in the downstairs room that was primarily the kitchen. I remember the crazy-patch quilt that covered him. Unable to speak, he talked with his eyes and made it understood he wanted Grace, who was between two and two-and-a-half years old and running all over the place, to sit beside him. So, Grandma sat her on a little straight chair beside Grandpa's pallet and they studied each other silently.

Grandma had broken at least one rib, and maybe more, in a fall. I believe she fell down the cellar steps. I recall that she was bedridden for some time in the downstairs room, where the organ was. She also had a crazy-patch quilt on her bed as the doctor examined her.

For a time, I was longing to be grown up. A 'grown up' was synonymous with 'a woman with a baby in her arms, on her left hip or at her breast.' One dark night, a man who was apparently a stranger, stopped at our house to stay the night. He was on his way from the farm of someone farther up the hills to Franklin, and he would continue his journey the following morning. Wanting to appear grown up, I persuaded Momma to let me hold the baby, Grace, on my lap while I was sitting on one end of the hearth. Daddy sat in front of the hearth, and the stranger at the corner, between the center and the end opposite me. Momma was working around the kitchen, Daddy and the stranger were talking and I felt very much like one of them…with a baby on my lap. When I suddenly decided that some wood needed to be pushed back farther into the fireplace, I stood Grace on the hearth and leaned toward the fire. At that moment, the whole spell was broken; I was a young un' again…Grace had been sleeping soundly on my lap, and when I put her down she could have fallen into the fire. Daddy spoke sharply to me, and Momma came to take Grace. Crestfallen, I left my place at the hearth.

Two little verses of a song that Daddy sang…now and then they remain with me:

> Me and my wife and my wife's dog,
> Crossed the creek on a hickory log.
>
> Me and my wife and my wife's pap,

Walked all the way from the Cumberland Gap.

And there was the song:
> I got a girl in the sourwood holler,
> Hey ho diddle dummy day;
> She won't come and I won't call her,
> Hey ho diddle dummy day.
>
> Git your dog and we'll go hunt 'er,
> Hey ho diddle dummy day;
> A few more jumps and I'll be with 'er,
> Hey ho diddle dummy day.

The trays on which we dried fruit in the summertime were set up on a sort of table that had legs about six feet high. Maybe the halved peaches were spread out on shingles; I'm not sure. I recall standing beside the drying scaffold one day when Fleet Rogers was there talking to some people…maybe Daddy, Momma, Aunt Mary and Uncle Avery. I was interested in his first name; it was so unusual. And although he paid no special attention to me, he was of an age that caused me to notice him.

Uncle Fred, Momma's brother, and his wife, were at our house with their little baby, Frieda. We were all wandering along between the corn field and the potato patch, and the adults were talking. Frieda started to crawl into a mass of potato vines that trailed down the side of the mound onto the path. I believe I leaned over and drew her back.

Fodder stacks dotted the corn field. Daddy and one or two other men were working furiously, trying to get all the fodder carried to shelter before the threatening sky began pouring rain. As the clouds grew blacker, I was called out to help. I worked along with them, carrying fodder that dragged on the ground beside me. I seem to remember a feeling of exhileration after the work was completed, which probably means that we were successful in 'bringing in the sheaves' before the cloudburst came.

There was a big tree on the lower part of Grandma Peek's land that was the source of awful contemplation. If we had to pass by it, we skirted it at some distance. Once in a while, if we felt exceptionally daring, we'd stay on the path, lower our heads, and dart under the tree. That was the 'panther tree' and one of our landmarks. The story went thusly: At dusk, one day, somebody's great aunt somebody (maybe it was Kate) was walking on the path, going to bring home some cows. As she trod beneath the tree, a great black panther that was lurking in the branches leapt upon her. She would have been torn to shreds had not her screams brought her husband, or someone, running from the nearby woods with his axe to save her.

One dream I had, which was of a common variety, has stayed with me because it's probably the first dream I had of that type. I dreamed I was running across the yard toward the house, being chased by a big bear. Just as I reached the front steps, I fell. With my arms outstretched, I tried desperately to put my hands on the bottom step, using it for support to raise myself. Straining every nerve and muscle, I groveled there until the bear was ready to pounce on me. With blessed relief, I awoke.

And there was the falling dream. I fell off a high mountain road, and dropped through space, past trees and rocks…awaking just before hitting the ground. The road I fell off was the one leading to the mill.

I had a cold, and Grandma Peek told Momma it might be due to the fact that I had gone to school without a cap on my head. Grandma had tried unsuccessfully to get me to wear a certain knit cap, with a ball at the peak, a short time previously. I balked so firmly because that cap wasn't to my liking that she finally had to let me go bareheaded. Momma told me that I must always mind what Grandma said thereafter.

One day as our cousin, Leona, came into the house from the spring, Florence, also a cousin, offered her a bread and butter sandwich. Leona took it readily and began eating it, but she hadn't gone far before she realized she had been duped; it was a lard sandwich.

On one very dark night, the men at Grandma Peek's house asked Leona if she'd go to the spring and get a bucket of water. She was afraid of the dark, which they all knew, and wouldn't go. When they tired of teasing her, they said they bet I wouldn't be afraid to go. I was simply horrified at the prospect, but they egged me on and it was in the form of a challenge. Trying to hide my absolute fear, I took a bucket (I think it was a two-pound lard tin with a wire handle that we kids ordinarily used) and stepped out the back door into the night. Some of them were standing at the door, watching me, and thereby blocking what light would have come out from the kerosene lamp in the room behind them. With their eyes upon me, I had to walk nonchalantly, with the darkness growing more dense with each step, to the spring. I stooped and filled my pail, and turned to walk back to the house. Employing every bit of control I had within me, I refrained from bolting and running toward the light shining behind the figures in the doorway. After an eon, I entered the door and set my pail down. I don't know whether any of them were aware that I had just died a thousand deaths at their hands.

I had just learned that it was incorrect to say, "I don't want nothing." One should say, "I don't want anything." Grandma's supper table was crowded with people sitting on the long side- benches and on chairs at the two ends of the table. Two or three times during the meal, someone asked me what else I'd care to have to eat. Since I was, of course, unaware of the reason for their solicitude, I felt very proper each time when I answered, "Anything, thank you."

We were annoyed several nights in succession by a flying squirrel that came to the same spot under the eves at the back of the house. It was next to the window of the upstairs bedroom where I was sleeping. The noise it made sounded like a pecking, or maybe it was the flapping of wings against the wood; anyway Daddy was trying to get rid of it. I think the weapon he used was the broom, but every time he'd get to the window and get it opened, the nuisance had disappeared. One night, I watched it as it flew away.

Momma and some woman from a neighboring farm were discussing the case of a third woman who couldn't swallow. The victim had had a quilt inserted in her throat, they were saying. I heard it and wondered. I visualized a crazy-patch quilt all wadded up and reposing in a woman's throat. I was rather puzzled as to how a big quilt could be confined in so small a space, but it had been said and I didn't doubt it. I also wondered just how that would help the poor woman to swallow, but some diversion arose and I didn't ponder very long on something that was beyond my comprehension. At a later date, I found out that it wasn't a quilt that was in the throat; it was a quill. I had never heard of the word at the time I had overheard the conversation about it, but when I inadvertently learned the word, the puzzling conversation came to my mind and was solved by my newly-acquired knowledge.

On repeated occasions, I screwed up the organ stool to the necessary height, climbed up on it, and played the organ in Grandma's downstairs bedroom. The song I played was one that Florence and Leona had taught me, and I accompanied myself vocally:

> There came a man a-ridin' by'
> Poor ole horse, you're goin' to die.
> If you die, I'll save yore skin,
> If you live, I'll ride you agin...
>
> Poor ole horse!

Someone gave us kids a dog, and we called him Rover. He was brown, or tan, and white; and he was of a mixture that included collie. One Sunday, the whole family returned home from church, and one of us soon discovered that Rover's house, which was set on the side of the house next to the chimney, was partly burned. And there was a deeply scorched spot, about three feet high, on the outside wall of our house. The burned portions of the dog's house and ours were, daddy concluded, caused by a spark that flew out of the chimney and lit on the dog's bedding, during our absence. The bedding was, I believe, still smoldering, and we doused water over everything. There was some observation to the effect that we were very fortunate to come home and find the house still standing.

One reason that Daddy allowed us to have the dog in the first place was that he might be helpful in keeping the chickens out of the gardens. But we discovered almost immediately that he was much more afraid of the chickens than they were of him. When we'd point at the straying chickens and say, "Sick 'em, Rover, sick 'em," he'd either wag his tail and look at us or he'd run in another direction.

I think his disobedience along that line was the reason Daddy used for giving him away.

One of the first proverbs I ever learned was: "Pride always goeth before a fall." I believe I was in the first grade. I was strolling across the school yard, pondering this bit of wisdom, paraphrasing it thusly: 'If you're proud, or bigotty, you might fall down.' I watched my step as I walked.

Grace and I were sitting on the steps outside Grandma's bedroom, and Grace stuck a bean up one of her nostrils and couldn't extract it. Either Virginia or I ran to get Grandma, who came and blew into Grace's mouth. The bean dislodged and fell out.

Leona and Florence, in their efforts to get ahead of one another in playing tricks, resorted to sewing up, with long basting stitches, the sleeves and neck of the dress that the victim had laid out to put on the following morning when she got out of bed. Once, the joke was played on me by someone. And once, I joined in the tricking by helping one of the girls sew up the bottoms of one of our boy cousin's trouser legs.

Aunt Harriet brought me a gorgeous little parasol one time when she visited us. I think it was on a Sunday, and I can see myself walking, with Virginia, out in the sunny barnyard. I was as proud as a peacock, shielding myself from the sun with my fancy pink parasol.

There was a black cat that resided in our barn and thrived on mice. She was Virginia's to claim, and when the cat had a half dozen kittens we were all thrilled. We went to the barn with Daddy to see them, and were heartbroken when he produced a tow-sack into which he placed all but one or two of the baby kittens. We knew what was in store for them. He also put a good-sized rock into the tow-sack, tied up the top, and we all headed for the creek. There he dropped the sack and its contents into the water and it sank immediately out of sight.

I knew Momma wasn't well, and that was why she slept in the screened porch. It was determined that a warmer climate would help her feel better and that we would join Daddy's brother, Uncle Lee, in sunny California. Our journey by train lasted five days. Little did I know that California would be where I would spend all the rest of my days.

Ventura

Ventura
January 6, 1927 – November, 1928
~Genevieve, 9 years old, Virginia, 7, Grace, 4~

Once we arrived in California, I believe we were at Uncle
Lee's and Aunt Ivory's only eighteen days before we
moved into our own new home. Daddy had bought a lot on
McFarland Drive and within that time a four-room house
had been thrown together for us. The lot was very deep and
the house was set near the back. Since the tract had been a
lemon orchard before subdivision, all the houses on the
street, including ours, had lemon trees surrounding them.
We still had a wood cook stove, and we used kerosene
lamps (Aunt Ivory gave us one, which I still have). There
was a cesspool on one side of the house with a privy built
over it. There were restrictions here: the cesspool had to be
so deep and lined with bricks or rocks. The vertical boards
that the walls of the house were composed of were stained
brown.

I was given a belt of about an inch width, and I put it
around my waist…over a dress that didn't necessarily need
a belt. It was the first time I had ever had a belt on and as I
was leaning on the picket gate in front of the house, I felt
that all the passers-by must be aware of my having it on.

After we were in the house for some time, an addition was
built on the west side of the house; that was the bathroom.
It contained a bathtub that stood on legs and a toilet bowl,
no wash basin. That toilet was a source of fascination. Even
Uncle Lee's toilet hadn't been so fancy. His was flushed by
pulling a chain, but ours merely required the pressing of a
handle. For the first few days, it saw a great deal of
unnecessary flushing.

Then came a washing machine, and it stood in the bathroom. Momma took in washing. The customers delivered and picked up their laundry. I believe it was all rough dry work; Momma also ironed shirts for some people. I recall one man's telling her how pleased he was with the job she had done on his shirts. She washed until her failing health forced her to give it up.

Daddy's work was with a contractor. He had something to do with a cement mixer, and one day he came home with his mouth injured…his lips bruised and swollen, and his front teeth so loose that they were near to falling out. He had been cranking the cement mixer, I believe, and was hit directly in the mouth when the crank got out of hand.

For a while Momma pitted apricots during the summer. Some women came by in a car and picked her up each day and brought her home in the afternoon. I went along sometimes and, with a paring knife that was furnished me, helped her fill her trays. On the way home from the shed one day, I was sitting in the back seat of the car with Momma and a couple of other women. Someone up in the front seat mentioned a woman by her first name; Ida So-and-So had done this or that. Momma asked, "Ida How-Much?" meaning "Ida Who… what was her last name?" The other women all laughed and one of them commented upon Momma's wit. The one at the wheel, I believe.

There was a huge gray angora cat that belonged to these people, or to someone nearby. When Tomasina, that was its name, wandered into our yard, we loved to play with her. I have a picture of Grace holding the cat, snuggling up to it.

The woman across the street had two irons and Momma had none. She gave one of them to Momma and it was in use at our house until we kids had some kind of trouble with the woman's children. I suppose it was a quarrel over some toy or other. After the squabble, anyway, the woman demanded her iron back, and it was given to her.

I don't know how many of Momma's friendships with the neighboring women were broken up by us kids. All the other children seemed to have so much bigger a selection of playthings, and we were so eager to get our hands on them. There was a quarrel among some of us at the Cheney's house over some of their play things. Virginia and I left their house and they followed us out into their yard. There, as we were departing, we had a lemon fight. We threw lemons at each other, with intent to hit our marks, until Virginia and I were out in the street.

Our first Christmas in Ventura sticks in my mind. I was up early in the morning to go to the kitchen where our stockings hung. It was cold and rainy. In fact, the rain had come in through the cracks in the walls and under the kitchen door. Either Momma or Daddy came out and sopped up the water from the floor. In the meantime, I was hardly aware of the dark, damp kitchen; I was going through my Christmas stocking. The only thing I can remember that it yielded was a beautiful little fountain pen, the size to fit a child's hand. It was pink with a half-dozen tiny flowers standing in relief around the top section of the pen. Aunt Hattie had sent it to me from North Carolina. In a letter that arrived shortly before Christmas, she had said that she had seen Santa Claus down town and had told him what we kids would like.

One Sunday afternoon before Virginia and I started to school in Ventura, the whole family went out for a walk. We walked all the way to the Avenue Grammar School, where we were to be sent. On the way, at the corner of Ventura Avenue and McFarland Drive, we looked at Mr.

McFarland's house. It was an impressive old structure, two stories tall and painted white, with trees and shrubs surrounding it. He owned the new subdivision and our street bore his name.

Aware of the great furor in the adult world, on May 26, 1927, Charles Lindbergh has flown solo across the ocean.

Virginia and I set out to walk from our house to Uncle Lee's one day. We were cautioned to watch the cars, walk on the shoulder of the highway, and look out for the steamrollers. The steamrollers were active in that vicinity because so many new streets in the subdivision were being paved. I recall walking along the dirt shoulder, bearing in mind the admonition concerning the steamrollers.

One time, on the way to the grocery store on the Avenue to get something for Momma, Virginia found a coin in the street. For a long time after that, when I was walking to the store, I kept my eyes on the ground, sending up a continuous running prayer, the while, that I would find some money.

There was peanut butter in our kitchen cupboard, too high for me to reach. When the house was quiet (Momma was either outside or lying down in the bedroom), I'd climb upon the draining board and reach into the cupboard for a teaspoon full of the delicacy that I was so fond of.

Before we had enough beds in the house to sleep the whole family, I slept in a crib. I touched the head and foot of it. Virginia slept on two chairs that were pushed together, face to face. I think Grace must have slept with Momma and Daddy. All in the same room.

The house swarmed with flies in the warm weather because there were no screens on the doors or the windows. Daddy paid Virginia and me at the rate of either a cent or a nickel for every hundred we killed with the swatter.

We had a garden to one side and in front of the house. I don't know what it consisted of besides tomatoes, but I remember making countless trips from the spicket to the tomato patch with pails of water on the days we had to water the garden. We had no rubber hose.

The three of us had whooping cough at one time. When we were kept in the house with it at first, Aunt Ivory came one day and brought some dresses that she had made for us. Mine was of a burnt orange voile. It was sleeveless, with lace around the armholes. And lace around the neck. There were two or three horizontal ruffles of about a foot's length in the front, between the waist and the hem. The ruffles overlapped one another and were also trimmed in lace. After we were able to be outside, with our whooping cough, we played in the front yard, still whooping.

To the right of us, past a couple of vacant lots where nothing but lemon trees stood, lived some people whose name was Peterson. I remember a song that was popular at that time which I believe I learned from hearing Mr. Peterson sing it. It went, in part:

> Make my bed and light my light;
> I'll arrive late tonight.
> Bye, Bye, Black Bird.

This same man came to our house on one or two occasions with a big pan full of hot biscuits that he had supposedly made.

I thoroughly enjoyed learning, and it was always gratifying to bring home a good report card. When we were learning our multiplication tables in school, I stayed awake every night for a while after I got into bed and repeated the multiplication tables to myself in a whisper, up through the twelves.

Momma made a black satin dress for me out of someone else's dress, maybe her own, to wear to school. At first, I liked it; the material felt so good and I liked the fit of it…tight at the waist with a gathered skirt. But I didn't wear it to school very long before I realized that I was out of place. Everyone else wore bright colors, gay prints and plaids. I became increasingly aware that we were poorer than some and that I had to wear what I had to wear.

We carried our lunch to school in paper pokes, and I would have given anything for a lunch pail like the more popular girls had. Some time later, I felt like an outcast though because I had to carry a lunch pail when the girls I most admired carried their lunches in paper bags. I guess children always want to do what the majority does. Convention is strong, and kids are sensitive about being in the minority groups.

I always enjoyed the singing class. We sang 'Deck the Halls with Boughs of Holly' and other Christmas songs. And I loved the color and atmosphere that one song seemed to impart to me. We harmonized to it:

> With clinking and clanking
> With beating drums and colors bright
> The circus procession
> Comes slowly into sight.
>
> Gay chariots, fair ladies

Bold horsemen from far distant lands
Pass by with gaunt camels
And elephants and bands.

The teacher came down the aisle, lowering her head as she passed the desk in front of me, and then my desk, to see how our row was doing with the alto. She couldn't hear our tones above the rest of the class except by lowering her ear. She spoke in approval as she passed my desk and I was singing the fourth line, "Comes slowly into sight."

There was a girl named Ella who lived at the end of our street near the Avenue. She and I got off the bus together, talking about who would come to whose house next. She asked me to come to her house, and I said, "I've been to your house twice in succession." I had just recently become acquainted the word and was consciously aware of the fact that I was using it.

From some forgotten source, I acquired a pin which I wore at the neck of my dress nearly every day. It was in the image of a ballerina, about an inch and a half tall. It was brass, but I called it gold; and the little dancing lady's costume was studded with about a dozen different colored stones.

Recess was over one day, and we pupils were just entering the classroom and sitting down at our desks when some girl told me, "Your sister fell off the bars and hurt her nose." I was greatly agitated at the news because I did not know what to do. My first impulse was to walk out of the classroom at once and go to the sick room where the girl had told me Virginia was lying, and which was almost adjoining the room I was in. But the teacher was just bringing the class to order and I obeyed her by giving my attention. Then I wanted to go up to the front of the room and ask the teacher if I could be excused, but I was so frightfully timid that I sat through the period...wondering constantly how badly Virginia was hurt, wondering if she had been taken home yet, feeling like a coward and a traitor for not leaving the room, excused or not, and going to her. I suffered agonies until I got home that afternoon. The school nurse had brought Virginia home and poor Momma had had a terrible shock at seeing her home from school early with her face bloody and discolored. I think it was fractured. She had stacked some bricks underneath the bars on the playground in order to stand on them to reach the bars. Then she pulled herself up and was doing all kinds of acrobatic stunts on the bar when she fell off and struck her nose on the bricks, knocking herself unconscious.

Virginia was always very agile and athletic, whereas I was so stiff and afraid of hurting myself that I couldn't even turn a cartwheel.

I had four 'boy friends' during the time that I was at Ventura Avenue Grammar School. They were Billy _____, Sherrill _____, Jefferson Davis and a Chinese boy named Makota. Makota sat across the aisle from me and we got along together very well. Democracy! He made a gift of a little ring one day...very similar to the one I had lost in the pine needles in Ellijay.

In my physical education class, we played 'Farmer in the Dell' and some other game where we joined hands, skipped around in a circle, and sang, "We'll catch a fox and put him in a box and then we'll let him go." Playing some kind of game one day that required running by turn, I fell and skidded on the ground. The indignity of it all was ghastly enough, but to add injury to insult, I fell on my bent-under right-hand wrist and sprained it. It was painful and I cried. Walking back toward the school building after the physical ed. class, in a small group of girls, one of them said, with a little air of triumph, "I fell down once and broke my back, but I didn't even cry." I believe my wrist was tightly bandaged with adhesive tape when I was telling Daddy at home that night about my fall. I told him, "A girl at school said she fell and broke her back, and she said she didn't cry." He asked, "Did you cry? Is that why she said that?" Unwilling to reveal injured pride, I answered, "No, she just said that"—implying she had said it without provocation.

We played baseball in the first semester of the fifth grade. I was up at bat waiting for the pitch, dreading the prospect of striking out again…as was my usual wont. I had not only my personal pride to worry about; there was the fact that girls who couldn't bat a ball were not welcome additions to their team. When the two captains would be choosing up sides, I'd be the last one chosen. I was always the cow's tail in every form of competitive sports. Anyway, there I stood, determined to try, but knowing it would be the same old story –'Three strikes and you're out.' At that moment, the sixth grade class was dismissed and the boys from the class, who seemed to be an awful lot older than I was, came yelling into the yard. When a couple of them saw me standing at the home plate, weighing my bat and touching it to the plate two or three times, they called out, "Hey, Wood Chopper, Wood Chopper." That was the term that meant they were aware I was up at bat; I was all the more desperate. I waited for the pitch, praying the while, "Let me hit it, let me hit it." I saw the ball coming, I swung, and I hit it! While I was running to first base, I was conscious of the most delicious sensation …a feeling of equality. My elation was some time in wearing off.

I think it was at the end of my fourth year of school when Mrs. Metcalf gave a party for the class. It was held on a lawn somewhere; it was probably at her home. We were all sitting on the grass, waiting for the refreshments, when she came out with the cake and ice cream. In the midst of the group, she said, smiling, "Angel Food for my angels"…and we were served the fluffiest and the whitest cake I had ever seen.

For days before that term ended, we kids talked about what teacher we would have the following year. For a while, there had been some talk of our coming back to Mrs. Metcalf the next year, and I was hoping fervently for just that. I couldn't bear to face the prospect of having to become acquainted with a new teacher, and I knew that whoever she might be she couldn't possibly compare with Mrs. Metcalf. There was some talk of our having Miss Horton the following term; and there were rumors that she had been known to stick pupils with pins when her temper was tried. I don't know how much exaggeration that was, but there was some foundation for the story because she had been called on the carpet for something by the principal, Miss Lawry. Miss Lawry impressed me at that time as being tall and raw-boned with a square stern face, but she wasn't as stern as her appearance. There was a feud of some kind between Mrs. Metcalf and Miss Horton, and if I remember correctly, Miss Horton won. I don't believe Mrs. Metcalf was there the following year.

When Grace started the first grade, I believe she too had a black dress. It was of cotton and was trimmed on the sleeves, around the neck and at the hem with pink embroidered feather-stitching. But she had dimples and a personality that overcame such minor afflictions as black dresses. She came home one day with the announcement that "I must have It." All the kids liked her, she said. ['It' referred to the actress Clara Bow, who was known as the 'It Girl.']

At the beginning of the new term, part of the school building was undergoing some alterations, and for a long while some students went to afternoon classes and some to morning classes. I went in the mornings, and when I'd get off the bus at Leighton Drive, one block south of our street, Virginia was always there waiting to get on the bus for her afternoon schedule. When I got home, Momma usually asked if I met Virginia at the bus stop and I answered in the affirmative. But one noon when she asked me that, I said I hadn't seen Virginia at the corner. Momma worried all afternoon until Virginia came home safely from school. I don't recall what had interfered with our meeting routine.

When Virginia and I were going to school together in the mornings, we always spent whatever small coins we had for 'Momma's Cookies' in the grocery store at the corner of Leighton and Ventura Avenue. These we ate while waiting for the bus or put them in with our lunch to have at noon.

There was a girl named Irene Arquette, one of my classmates, whom I sometimes played with after school. I was aware that she looked different in some way or other from the average person. The only peculiar characteristic that I can remember now that she had was an olive complexion. She had gray eyes and dirty blond hair. It was undoubtedly her coloring that appeared unusual to me.

In the first half of the fifth grade, I handed in a composition along with the rest of the class, and the teacher made an example of me by telling the class that my composition was a perfect paper. She held it up so that everyone could see how neat it was, margins and all. Even though I always found it very gratifying to have my work praised before the class, I was somewhat worried that it might arouse the others to that hated reaction that impels them to dub brighter students 'teacher's pet.' Anyway, in this case, when the teacher commented upon my 'perfect paper,' someone spoke up "I thought you said that nobody's assignment was ever *perfect* and that you didn't expect it to be." The teacher said, yes, that was right and that this otherwise-perfect paper did, indeed, lack a period at the end of the last sentence in the last paragraph.

There was a cute little blond, blue-eyed boy that I admired immensely in the fifth grade. He lived on Leighton Drive, one block over. He wandered past our house one day after school and luckily I was in the yard. We sat side by side on the curb for a while, talking about whatever kids talk about. We ended up by my dragging out of him what I wanted to hear. With a stick, we had drawn a diagram of the seating arrangements of our classroom in the dirt on the street in front of us. We were naming off the ones who sat here and there. Finally I asked him who is favorite girl was in the room, and after a little study he said, "The girl in the third seat from the front, in the second row from the left", and he pointed with the stick to my seat in the diagram. When he wanted to know who my favorite boy was, I hemmed and hawed and couldn't bring myself to tell him. I think I said I would tell him the next day. He went home shortly thereafter, and I went into the house. I figured that since I didn't have the nerve to tell him verbally that he was my favorite I would write his name on a little piece of paper and hand it to him at the bus corner the following morning. I got my paper and pencil, but didn't know definitely how to spell his name. Not wanting to divulge my secret to Momma, I called out the window to where she was in the side yard, "Momma, I'm writing down the names of the kids in my room. You spell Evelyn e-v-e-l-y-n, don't you?" She answered, yes, that was right. Then I asked, "How do you spell Clifford?" She told me, and I wrote it down on my little piece of paper. I carried it with me the next morning, but never found an opportunity to give it to him; the whole thing was soon forgotten.

Momma gave a birthday party for Virginia, the only event I can recall that ever furnished cognizance of any of our birthdays. I don't remember who nor how many were invited, but I recollect wandering around in the yard munching jelly beans, chewing licorice sticks and drinking lemonade…conscious of the fact that the party atmosphere was lacking.

Unhappiness in those impressionable years has left with me an abhorrence of the odors of tar and of new telephone or light poles, both of which were omnipresent in that new subdivision where the streets were being laid and the poles erected. And a strong antipathy toward the odor or taste of licorice, which we ate in long rope form, during that period.

We ate countless lemons, doctored with salt. And we filled lugs with them for selling.

It was practically no time in finding that I spoke a different tongue from people here. Until I learned the new language, I was often embarrassed by other kids' reactions to my southern speech. I had to learn to translate 'poke' into 'sack,' 'tow sack' into 'gunny sack,' 'time' into 'turn,' 'bigotty' into 'smart' or 'haughty,' and 'spell' into 'while.' And numerous other words and phrases I had to learn. One evening, I went into the home of a little girl down the street when her parents were sitting down to supper (or dinner). The mother told my little playmate to sit down at the table, and the girl made some kind of contrary remark. Her mother turned to me and asked, "What would your mother say if you talked to her like that?"
I answered, "She'd tell me not to be so saucy." The woman caught her husband's eye across the table, smiled and

winked. I wasn't embarrassed that time because I felt that she wasn't being malicious, but I realized at once that I should have said 'sassy' instead of 'saucy.'

Some portrait studio sent out a photographer to our house who took pictures of us three kids in the yard. We were standing on the plowed-up ground and a big clod of dirt at my feet photographed with a striking resemblance to a frog. And due to some defect in the film or to poor printing, there appeared a bump on one of my legs that resembled a boil. These little illusions didn't do much to damage the over-all appearance of the photograph, however; the expression on my face was anything but one of congeniality. My chopped-off bangs hung unevenly about my eyebrows, and beneath them my eyes looked out so dark and woebegone that frogs at my feet and boils on my legs couldn't have done much in the way of detracting from the whole gloomy aspect of the photograph.

Uncle David arrived at our house and he slept in the front room. He was a constant tease, but he was entertaining and good looking and I liked him. Sometimes at the table, after a meal, he'd want a cigarette and would ask, "Who'll bring my cigarettes off the table?" If he had been teasing us during the meal, Virginia and Grace got even with him by sitting still. After a moment, I'd go and get the package off the table beside his bed. On one occasion, he rewarded me with a penny…probably not to make me feel good, but to make Virginia and Grace feel bad.

He was going with a girl there, and once or twice we kids had a wonderful time peeking out and watching the two of them neck as they sat in his tan convertible coup in front of the house. It seems that the girl was some distant relation to some of us because she knew Momma and Daddy, and she came in the house with Uncle David after they finished snuggling and kissing. It was a curious act to watch and it made me fell oddly stimulated. I wondered vaguely how it would feel when I would try it someday.

One day after school, Uncle David drove Virginia and me to a dentist on Main Street in Ventura. We were both supposed to have some dental work done, and I had Virginia go into the dentist's office first. I think she was in tears when she entered, and by the time she came out I was in such a nervous state of apprehension that I was in tears. And I refused to enter the office. Neither the dentist nor Uncle David could persuade me and they finally gave up. We got into the car and went home again, with me crying nearly all the way. I knew I should have gotten into the chair for my own good while I had been subjected to the opportunity, and I was upset at having had so little self-discipline. I knew I would have to go sooner or later, and the prospect of having to anticipate it when I could have had it over with by then made me all the more unhappy.

One night, Daddy, Momma, Uncle David and we kids all went in his coupe to the Baines' house. We three kids were stuck behind the seat in some way so that we were half-sitting and half-standing. At the Baines' everybody except Momma had a good deal to drink. She had nothing, and the others, in their state of temporary hilarity, were making a point of her sobriety and singing to her, "Oh, Eliza, Eliza Jane." On the way home, with the top of the car down, we three kids were perched up in the breeze; and I, for one, felt very insecure at riding with Uncle David.

I was sick unto death practically with something that caused me to have a very high fever. In the night, I was delirious and was crying out unconsciously. I was having a delirious vision of newspapers. There were scads of them, and it seems as if they were on legs, moving en masse in front of me. Then, in my helplessness, they seemed to be heading for me, like some evil thing, with some of their folded pages flapping. Daddy, upon hearing my screaming about newspapers, hurried into the room and I recall lying there and telling him about my visions while he tried to bring me out of the semi-conscious state.

Sometimes, there were eerie moaning sounds in the hills to the side of our house that gave me the goose pimples. The howling came from a roaming coyote and sounded like a human cry.
But one night the crying we heard on the hillside was the anguished outpouring of some woman who was roaming up there in the darkness alone. I think Daddy went out if front of the house to investigate and came back saying that a man had climbed the hill to bring the woman down.

In the daytime, we kids often lay down with our arms at our sides, on the slope of the hillsides, and rolled down to the bottom...down the incline that was cushioned with tall green supple grass.

I believe it was in 1928 that the Hickman kidnapping took place. I read in the newspapers from day to day of how parts of her horribly mutilated body were found, wrapped in blood-soaked newspapers. This ghastly and inhuman activity made my nights miserable for a long time. I had been used to sleeping with either Virginia or Grace, on the outside of the bed next to the door of the room, but I was so horribly frightened of the darkened room when I couldn't free my mind of the murder I had been reading about that I began sleeping on the inside of the bed, next to the wall. I think I was cunning enough to avoid mentioning to my bed partner the reason for wanting to change sides; I knew that such an admission would make her refuse to sleep on the outside ...and justifiably. For different reasons, I didn't mention to Momma how fearful I was. I suppose that was because I didn't want to give way to my fears with anyone else's knowledge.

Frequently in the afternoon, Momma had us kids go to the over-grown vacant lot next door or to the foot of the hills and pick mustard greens for dinner.

During the same period, I often lay flat on my back at night, with my hands clasped upon my chest and my legs stretched straight down. In this attitude, with no thought of any earthly thing on my mind, I'd say to myself, "Right now I'm perfect." And I imagined that God, the ubiquitous, would be taking stock of the fact that I was, at the particular minute, perfect. It's peculiar that I assumed a perfectly symmetrical position of the body was the basic part of such perfection. Probably was due to a methodical mind.

Also at that time, I put myself through a phase of passiveness. I suppose I figured that way I would be unable to do anything wicked. When Virginia and Grace would be scrapping, verbally or physically, in the back yard, I'd sit on the step and watch them, refusing to interfere and refraining from taking sides…even mentally. I'd tell myself that one of them was as good and as right as the other and I'd let them go at it. Once in a while, I admit, I felt an intense dislike toward one or the other of them, but I'd tell myself that I loved them both the same. During that period, I believe I avoided having any squabbles of my own too.

There was another streak of the earache. Momma put me to bed and while I was crying with the pain, she put warm oil into my right ear and also heated the flat iron and wrapped it in a cloth so that I could keep it next to my ear. She asked me if I had stuck anything inside my ear and I told her I had put a pencil inside it at school. She said, "Don't ever put anything smaller than your finger in your ear."

Aunt Hattie, Momma and we kids had been gleaning walnuts from the ground up in the foothill orchard. The pickers had already been through the orchard and we felt that we were entitled to whatever was left. That was honest. When we returned to the house, Momma sat down on the first chair she encountered, which was in the kitchen. She sat down so abruptly and looked so strange that we were at once aware that something was wrong. As I stood looking at her, she closed her eyes and started leaning to the left. I believe it was Aunt Harriet who caught her before she toppled from the chair and got her to bed. Momma had fainted, and I was alarmed. I was aware before that that she was weak and had to stay in bed a great deal, but I didn't know what her sickness was.

I had gotten a hold of some books about dogs. All breeds of dogs were pictured, and there was a little story of the background of each breed printed underneath their respective pictures (drawings, not photographs). With my paper and pencil I sat on the ground, leaning against a walnut tree trunk, and drew dogs, sketching them from the book…disdaining to trace them. It was a warm and dusty day, and I was happy. Although I recall this incident distinctly, I find it difficult to place chronologically. I can't remember whether it took place in this Ventura period or whether it happened in later years. This, I attribute to the fact that I was so wrapped up in what I was doing that I was unaware, for the time, of any unpleasantness in my world. I was in another universe, expressing myself in drawing…I was in the various lands where the dogs in question originated. It was one of those brief and infrequent afternoons when I was happy and was simultaneously aware of happiness.

I was the proud owner of a new pair of shoes, and I was so careful to keep them from getting scratched that I refrained from walking on the gravel of the street. I walked on the curbstone. Since I had some difficulty in balancing myself on its six-inch width, I had Virginia and Grace walk on either side of me and hold my arms.

We played in a gigantic stack of hay that was located on the un-built side of Comstock Drive, one block behind our house.

I believe our friendship with the Bogner family started one evening when we were out walking in the late daylight after dinner. Walking down our street, our family of five encountered the Bogner family of three…Mr. and Mrs. and Marcella who was about four years old. We began going to each other's house and became quite neighborly. At their house, we kids were astounded to see Marcella eat mayonnaise by the spoonful; none of us had become accustomed to it.

We kids played on their front lawn in the afternoon (on Leighton Drive) with Marcella's playthings. She had a little toy store set-up that I admired immensely. There were shelves on which I placed the various canned goods and other groceries; and the others acted as customers, using the little tokens that were marked in various denominations of coin.

I had become aware of the advertising slogans for various products; among these Pet Milk's slogan, 'From Contented Cows.' One summer evening when the Bogners and we were strolling down Comstock Drive, I noted the manner in which Daddy was walking toward the west, apparently at peace with the world in the fleeting hour separating day from night, and in a moment of silence I spoke out, "Daddy, you look just like a contented pig." For an instant, I was in doubt as to whether I had spoken wisely, but everybody chuckled at the simile.

Marcella contracted some severe type of fever, and we weren't allowed to go to her house for a long time. While she was fever-ridden, her dirty blond, straight hair fell out, and when we next saw her she had a short growth of curly hair. We kids were amazed, and I rather wished that I could have a fever so that my hair might grow in curly. I knew the seriousness of the fever, but I wanted curly hair that badly. I also would have considered trading my soul for blue eyes like those that a beautiful little girl had whom I played with sometimes on our street.

We three kids were in the back yard, near the door, when Momma appeared at the door with a wet mop in her hands. Evidently we had carried dirt onto the cleaned kitchen floor and she had to go over part of it. What impressed me was how upset Momma was because it was so unusual. And it was frightening because she was on the hysterical side as she scolded us. Her features seemed to change shape and her face was distorted as she leaned against the door and tears came to her eyes. Greatly disturbed, I began to cry and ran across the yard and disappeared into the erstwhile privy. Since we had had a toilet installed in the house, the privy had been moved to one side so that the cesspool could be covered over. The privy now housed a large collection of rags I crouched there for a long time, muffling my sobs in the pile of rags, with the door closed against any possible interloper. I heard Momma calling me, but I couldn't answer her. I knew something was horribly wrong even though I hadn't willfully tracked dirt from the barren yard onto the kitchen floor, I cursed myself for causing Momma trouble, and I felt the deepest compassion for her swell up in me. At long last, I disengaged myself from the enveloping rags and went into the house. There, I put my arms around Momma and told her how sorry I was.

Our new stucco house was erected in front of our old brown-stained structure, and the new house was salmon pink! It had hardwood floors, a fireplace, fancy light fixtures…but it was bare, except for a few old pieces of furniture we had carried in from the other house; namely, some straight chairs and a table and some bedsteads. We were proud of this classy new home and anticipated seeing it furnished . But that was not to be our meed.

In this period, Momma frequently made celery soup, something we had never had before, and I liked it very much.

Uncle Willie, Daddy's brother, came out from North Carolina and I learned that he was blind in one eye because a piece of steel had flown into his eye sometime previously. One evening, Daddy, Uncle Willie, and a couple of other men were sitting in a semicircle in our front room (no bed in the living room here; there were three bedrooms) and talking. I walked up behind one of the men, not paying much attention to which one it was, but thinking vaguely that it was Uncle Willie. I leaned on the back of the chair, taking in the conversation and chewing my gum laboriously. The head of the man in the chair moved with an annoyed gesture at having gum chewed in such proximity to his ear. Feeling embarrassed, I deliberately chewed my gum with additional gusto, and the head swung around to reprimand me. Surprise covered my face when I saw that it was Daddy's chair I was standing behind, and I knew immediately that I shouldn't have been so bold as to increase the noise of my gum chewing. There was a stern look, and maybe a rebuke, and I was glad to make my exit.

Ojai

Ojai (pr: Oh Hi!)
November 1928 – February 1, 1931
~Genevieve, almost 11 years old,
Virginia, 9½, Grace, 6~

Our first residence in Ojai was 603 Emily Street, just off
Summer Street. We rented a brown-stained, four-room-and-
a-bath, house. To the rear of the house, was some lush
acreage which in the spring was intoxicating to the senses.
Wild flowers grew in profusion…lupines, golden poppies,
Indian paint brushes, and countless others.

> Paint brush, paint brush, Indian paint brush,
> Do the Indians paint with you?
> Children, children, I'm not certain,
> But I almost think they do.

The ground was cushioned with a short, luxurious grass,
and there were little ponds of water where we filled jars
with tad-poles (people called them pollywogs) to take home
and observe their metamorphosis. On a couple of occasions
we (in conjunction with Mrs. Fischer) packed picnics and
wandered farther away than usual to enjoy them.

Mrs. Fischer was our neighbor on our right. Mrs. Louis A.
Fischer, that is. She was a rightious woman, at whose
instigation we started attending Sunday school again. In
Ventura, we hadn't gone. When the church bells rang on
Sunday mornings, she would start chanting in rhythm with
them, "Come, Paul. Come, Paul." He was her only child
and was Grace's age. We rather enjoyed this modern
Sunday school where movies were shown as the primary
attraction. Educational religious reels. Their church was the

Presbyterian, so we Southern Baptists were sent to our own Sunday school once in a while.

We three kids had chicken pox simultaneously. Momma worked with us, trying to keep us from scratching and thereby creating scars.

One rainy morning, Daddy escorted us to school to get us enrolled. We sloshed along through the rain and mud toward Nordhoff Union Grammar School. There were fear and trembling in my gait. I abhorred the thought of entering a new school. I was not forward enough to make friends easily, and I hated being unpopular. We arrived at the principal's (Mrs. Sheldon's) office and she directed us to our respective classrooms. I entered Miss Crowder's room with my tail between my legs, but holding my head up and trying to appear at ease.

Miss Crowder's name was Frances, and she said that in college she had often been thought to be a boy until her presence proved otherwise. The idea was that her name was frequently being misspelled as Francis. I was in the fifth grade when I entered Nordhoff Grammar, and there I met a roomful of students with whom I was destined to finish high school, after some moving around in the interim. There were Sophia Scherer, Kathryn Williams, Della Mae Hart, Ardythe Tagley, Theodore Haegar, Preston Wickman and many others.

On Summer Street, I saw Earl Taylor for the first time, with his parents. He was four or five years older than I was, and he appeared to be grown up from where I stood. The night I met him, he sat in the back seat of his parent's car. Some mention was made of how he had saved considerable money from some work he had been doing. They were stopping by to see the Fischers for a few minutes, and the next time I saw him I was in high school.

We had a small cubicle known as a breakfast-room to one side of the kitchen. In it was a little table one end of which was attached to the wall with hinges and the other end of which was supported by a folding leg. One time, Grace accidentally kicked the folding leg inward, and within very short order our meal was on the floor. Among the other foods, there were canned apricots involved.

At this same table, we often played school when it was raining or dark outside. I was always the teacher and I gave lessons in arithmetic and spelling to Virginia and Grace. We went through the whole procedure of correcting papers, etc., and I often had to use persuasion to keep them at their lessons in a school-room manner.

At this point I began to read. Great vistas of a world that was hitherto undreamed of opened up, after I acquired a public library card. I read every minute of the time that I wasn't called upon to do something else, starting out with Pinocchio, Pied Piper of Hamlen, Children's Magazine published by Rand-McNally, Sunday school literature, etc. I was invariably interested in knowing the author's name; and when I found out that the issues of magazines had no author's name on the cover, I considered the publisher's name to be the next-best person to whom to give credit.

In April, 1929, we moved to another brown-stained house on Fulton Street. It had white window sashes. And it was ours; Daddy had bought it from a Mr. Faure...was buying it, that is. There was a vast expanse of lawn in the front of the house, which we watered by carrying endless pails of water from the faucet at the front of the porch. And that was how we watered the foot-high hedge that grew alongside the driveway. We were once again subjected to the use of a privy, which was set very near the back door. The neighbors on our left were named Trout.

This house was closer to the school than the previous one, and we came home for lunch. Until we obtained a stove for the kitchen, or until we had the gas turned on (whichever caused the delay), Momma cooked all our meals over the fire in the fireplace. For lunch, she often gave us eggs poached in milk. I remember how flushed her face was as she squatted on the hearth, cooking.

Daddy acquired a black and white chow dog for us, and we called him Teddy. Sometimes he perturbed us by jumping upon us and acting as a dog is wont to do with another dog. When he gave Grace that particular tail-end action, she concluded that it was because he "likes my pink dress." We thought he would be cured of chasing cars after he had his foot run over while indulging in that particular pastime, but it didn't seem to convince him.

I was subject to nose bleeds frequently that summer. Momma used to stop them by applying cold compresses to the back of my neck. The trouble was blamed on the hot weather.

My primary outdoor diversion then was playing jacks. I played by the hour on the Willingham's front porch. Wesley Willingham was my boyfriend temporarily. I was very eager to get hold of a note-book ring that he had. I needed it and had no way of getting one, so I had his sister Alice ask him for it for me.

Alice was twelve or thirteen years old and she was beginning to develop in the bust. I remember noticing, when she wore a dress with a three cornered tear, that blue

veins showed through the skin. I asked Momma why I
wasn't beginning to grow like Alice was.

Late one afternoon, Daddy came home drunk. He lay on the
bed and moaned pitifully. Evidently he had been expected
to bring home a loaf of bread when he came, but since he
didn't bring it, Momma sent me across the street to borrow
one from Mrs. Willingham, cautioning me not to tell why
we found it necessary to borrow it.

Aunt Hattie, who worked in Inglewood at the time, came to
visit us now and then. One evening, I went to bed knowing
that she would arrive later. Since she was to sleep with me,
I went to sleep with the idea in mind that I must keep to my
own side of the bed in order to leave room for her. I
overdid it a little, to the extent, in fact, where I fell out of
bed. While falling I was under the impression that she had
kicked me out. But when I hit the floor and awoke, I saw
that she hadn't arrived yet.

In my class at school, each pupil was to print his name on a
large folder. This folder was to contain our art work. I spent
a long time in printing my name, GENEVIEVE, in big
block letters on one line, centering it carefully. On the line
below, I started my last name. Seeing that just plain
HENRY was going to be off center, I put in an extra letter
to balance it properly. It ended up as HENERY.

School term was over in early June, and I worried for a
long time in advance about what I would wear on the last
day of school. I was under the impression that everyone
would dress up a little for the last day, so I wore my
dressiest dress. I didn't really want to wear it because I
knew it would be inferior to some of the other girls' best
dresses. But when I arrived at school, I discovered with
horror that no one else had worn anything special. I would

have been so much happier to have on my most ragged dress. I crept around all morning, feeling horribly conspicuous, knowing that I stuck out as someone who had tried unsuccessfully to dress up. The only remark that was made at all about my apparel was that my slip showed. I adjusted that by tying a knot in the wide shoulder band. It seemed that the time would never arrive when I could go home for lunch, not for the sake of the lunch, but because I was dying to get that dress off. Just before lunch-time, the teacher commented upon what a pretty dress I was wearing. I thanked her, but not cheerfully because I knew she was being kind. It seems that the day to dress up was the first day of school, not the last.

When Virginia's birthday arrived in June, Mrs. Fischer invited all of us over to her house to celebrate with Paul, whose birthday was just a day before or after Virginia's. She baked a big cake with a few coins folded into the dough. The first piece of cake was served to Virginia and she discovered that her slice contained a dime.

Mrs. Fischer gave Momma five dollars. She herself couldn't afford it, of course, but we were desperately in need of it, so she took it out of her tithe money which she was saving for the church. She said she figured that God would see that she was using it for a worthy purpose and not censure her for failing to give it to the church.

During the summer, when Mrs. F was at our house one day, she told us that she had something for us that would make our 'eyes pop out.' Whatever it was, she didn't have it with her. It was at home, but she would bring it over soon. We had no idea what it could be, but when she brought over six dresses (two for each of us) sometime after that, we reacted very badly. Our eyes didn't 'pop out.' To the contrary, we showed almost no gratitude for the great amount of time and work she had put into them. We needed and wanted dresses desperately, but we were so awfully disappointed in them that we found it impossible to act overjoyed. They were made out of scraps and remnants, to which we had no objection. But we saw instantly that the styles were very different from what our class-mates wore, and we were unhappy. Momma must have been horribly embarrassed and disappointed in our behavior. One of my dresses had large cape sleeves. Incidentally, liking the dresses or not, we wore them until they were worn out.

The McPhersons lived across and down the street from us. The children were Floyd, Evelyn and Charlotte. I worked for a while for Mrs. M. I cleaned house, ironed and did odd jobs. I was paid a quarter after each stint. When I told Momma how I had earned one particular quarter, she didn't allow me to work for Mrs. M anymore. I had used a broom to sweep a rug, about a nine-by-twelve one, and Momma explained to Mrs. M that she was afraid that type of work was too strenuous for me. It was almost as if Momma were visualizing how it would affect her, in her weak condition, if she herself should attempt that type of sweeping. Or, I suppose it was that she didn't want me to be breathing in all the dust I was raising while sweeping.

The packing house, less than a mile away, discarded tons of oranges that were not quite up to specifications. These were dumped in a great heap on the side of a slope. We used to go to the mountains of oranges and pick up all we could find that were free of mold and take them home.

There were some oleander bushes in the field behind our house. They were beautiful and we longed to pick them, but we were admonished against it because they were poisonous. Cows had been known to die after eating them.

One time when I was on Mrs. McPherson's porch with her, she gazed out at the tops of the mountains bounding the Ojai Valley (The Nest, in Indian) on the Southeast and said she wondered what was on the other side of the mountains. Without hesitation, I said that I had been on the other side of them. When I made the statement, I was of the opinion that Ventura was on the other side; but when she asked, "What is over there?" I hardly knew what to answer, for I knew that she had been back and forth between Ventura and Ojai more than I had and if Ventura *were* on the other side she would know it. So I answered, "It's the same on the other side as they are on this side."

Aunt Hattie was going with Fred Lawton at the time. When she came up from Inglewood, she'd bring him to our house with her often. He always brought us cookies and other goodies. Sometimes, we'd go for a ride with them in his car. His tactics in wooing included making an impression upon her three nieces. (That was a natural action, so if you ever read this, Harriet, don't feel that I'm being offensive.) One Sunday afternoon when we three kids sat in the back seat of the car, riding down the main street through Ojai, Aunt Hattie and Mr. Lawton asked us if we'd like to have some ice cream. Simply dying for want of it, and longing to answer in the affirmative, I firmly said, "No, thank you". And Virginia and Grace followed suit. We had always been discouraged from allowing people to give us things. Perhaps it was the pride of the poverty-stricken. Of course, while we insisted that we wouldn't care for any ice cream at all, we were hoping wildly that the car might stop, against our wishes, at the very closest ice cream store. In some instances, when events did take that turn, it was slightly embarrassing to be eating ice cream avidly after having so firmly denied that we wanted it. But with the ice cream in hand, the embarrassment wasn't insufferable.

On October 29th, 1929, Aunt Hattie stood in our bare and ugly living room, wearing a lovely blue transparent velvet dress. Her hair, bright auburn and wavy, hung long. She stood hand in hand with Uncle Fred, and a preacher had come to the house to marry them. Our family of five was the only spectators.

The school term had started again and I was in the sixth grade. There was one Walter Mazerrio in whom I was very interested.

At the end of that year, we lost our house. Mr. Faure said the bank was forced to foreclose on us because we were in arrears in payments. It was another failure for Daddy, and I felt his anguish deeply. I didn't care for the house; I knew it was a miserable shack. But I was shaken by the realization that Daddy had not succeeded in what he had set out to do…namely, to provide his family with a home of its own.

We had to move again; this time it was to a house on Grand Avenue, in December 1929. There were three houses on the lot, owned by Mr. and Mrs. Hagan. One house stood on the front of the lot, and two behind it. They were all painted green…a welcome change from our usual brown abodes. We moved into the rear house on the left, and the Hagans occupied the one on the right of us. Here, we three children slept in the bedroom and Momma and Daddy had the screened porch. There were also a kitchen and bathroom.

Mr. Hagan was old and rather stooped, and very wrinkled. He drove a convertible Ford, a gray coupe. Mrs. Hagan lived in a wheel-chair. She was more aged than Mr. H. and she had a sharpness about her that characterized her appearance as well as her make-up. Her face was edged…a beak-like nose, a precisely drawn mouth, and small quick eyes. Over the bone structure, her skin was tautly drawn.

The skin looked like that on a roasted turkey...of a brownish, parchment-like texture that had grown oily from lack of cleansing. Her nervous boney hands were active constantly, and they were hardened and calloused from twenty years of grasping and rolling the wheels of her chair. And her mind was alert; she chattered endlessly and her wit was lively. She did all the work that was done in the house. The rooms were always neat and orderly, but since she was unable to combat the grease and dust, they accumulated in layers in the hard-to-get-to areas. She cooked and washed dishes while sitting in her wheel-chair, she boiled and washed clothes on a low stove, she pushed the dust mop over the linoleum with one hand while wheeling herself with the other, she made the bed by rolling herself from one side to the other. This indomitable old lady scolded raucously at the radio when an announcer would start to advise her to buy this or that for such and such. She knew we found her ranting amusing so she colored up her terms of denouncement when we were around. She sang for us eagerly, going through chorus after chorus of 'Billy Boy,' her voice reaching a strident pitch when she came to, 'Sheeeee's a young thing and cannot leave her Mother.'

Mrs. Hagan gave us pennies from time to time for going to the store. And she let us keep the refunds on bottles that we returned. She wore her graying hair in a bun, drawn back severely from her face. Her hair, like the rest of her, clothes and all, had an appearance of greasiness about it. Her long dresses that came down over the high-topped shoes, into which her long-handled underwear was tucked, always had spots on the lap. Her long imprisonment in the wheel-chair was due to an accident she had while on her honeymoon, a day or so after her marriage to Mr. Hagan. She fell and broke her hip, and since she was at the time of her marriage an elderly woman the bones never knitted sufficiently for her to walk again.

By this time, Momma was bedridden much of the time, and I was doing a lot of the housework and part of the cooking. I remember only one time that I displayed resentment and rebellion against my lot. It was when Kathryn Williams, whom I had come to idolize, came to my house after school one afternoon and called me from the yard. I told Momma that I was going out to play with Kathryn for a little while, and she said with gentleness and firmness that I couldn't, that I would have to start supper. I was a little sick with disappointment because it wasn't usual for Kathryn to come and ask me out. I stood with my nose pressed against the screen on the porch where Momma was in bed and explained to Kathryn that I had to work. My unhappiness with the circumstances was voiced only when I said, "Oh, Momma, I want to."

I tried to copy every little trait that I admired so much in Kathryn. I began to roll my upper lip when I smiled because that's how her short upper lip operated. Her hair was brown and naturally wavy. I was very fortunate in one respect…that was that my hair was also brown. But I went through a lot of anguish in attempting to make my hair wavy like hers. When we were walking home from school through a very strong wind one day, I said I hated the wind. She said, "I like it." I can still visualize her with her head up and her hair maintaining its wave as we bucked the wind. I said, "I know why you like the wind," and she asked, "Why?" "Because," I told her, "your hair still stays wavy." I had spent the whole day pampering a slight crook in my hair that I had managed to obtain by rolling one strand around my finger and sleeping on that side of my head the night before. After that, I tried to get a wave in my hair by soaking it with olive oil. It took several shampoos to remove the oil, and I tried several times before Momma told me that just plain water wouldn't remove it; I had to use soap. Again, I raked together a few pennies and bought some flaxseed. I mixed it with water and applied the slimy solution all over my head. That way, I managed to procure a slight semblance of a wave in the front which disappeared entirely the first or second time I combed it. These were only a few of the tricks I tried upon the advice of various schoolmates.

I had always held in contempt all manner of rain-coats. I would rather get wet than don any of them. But when Kathryn wore a smartly belted rain-coat in the inclement weather, I saw that I had had the wrong impression of rain-coats until then. Suddenly, I wanted a real rain-coat so badly that I went to Sprague's Dry Goods Store and priced every one in stock, knowing that I would never have one, of course. I never even mentioned my longing for one to Momma or Daddy.

Kathryn and I took turns buying Milky Way candy bars for each other at noon time. It wasn't every day that I had a dime for such purposes, so time would usually lapse before I was able to come through with my turn at treating. Milky Way was a new bar, and it was delectable. It was also the cause of my losing my right thumbnail. While throwing a Milky Way wrapper into one of the push openings in a waste container at school, I caught my thumb and mashed it so that I was sick at my stomach.

One of the little stories I heard Aunt Hattie tell Momma during this period was about a young lady and her gentleman friend who were making polite conversation on a summer's eve. She said, "Aren't the stars multitudinous tonight?" And he answered, "Yes, and plenty of 'em too."

Momma lost her wedding ring, which was a plain wide gold band. It was worn thin and the edge, in one or two places, had worn in toward the center of the circlet. She was very upset at having lost it and concluded that it must have slipped off her thin finger into the toilet bowl. I was the happiest person in the world when on Easter morning I found her ring. I was happy because I knew it would make her happy. I came across it while rummaging through a corrugated box full of linens that was in the bedroom.

There was a frightful electric storm, and I couldn't find a spot to hide where I felt safe. I went running to the screened porch where Momma lay in bed, and she advised me not to touch the iron work of the bedsteads. I started to crawl under her bed, but she reminded me of the bed springs. I was shunning our cat which seemed determined to follow me at that crucial moment, for I had heard stories of how cats were good conductors for electricity.

It was play day at school. We were to engage in athletic contests with the pupils of San Antonio School who were our visitors. Our class lined up and sang to them: "How do you do, visitors, how do you do? Is there anything that we can do for you? We are mighty glad you came, and we hope you feel the same. How do you do, visitors, how do you do?" Frances Lambert headed the San Antonio students in replying to our musical query.

Then there was Arbor Day, when our student-body lined up along the railed side of the corridor to sing a song that we had all practiced for the occasion and to see the ceremony of a tree planting.

We three kids were among others in the school who were given free milk (a half-pint bottle) every morning at the ten o'clock recess. I detested the fact that it was free and that under-privileged and undernourished children included me, but I was crazy about milk and drank it like a glutton. Virginia disliked milk, free and otherwise, and tried to find ways of disposing of it every morning.

One of my favorite classes was Folk Dancing, which was supervised by Mrs. Kingman. She was a likeable and eccentric little old woman who was very agile and up on her lore. Our class was held outside on pleasant days and in the 'old building' on rainy days. We danced all types of peasant dances, and one of my favorite was the 'stick dance.' The only time that I would rather have dropped dead than go through the dance routines was when we had to hold hands and form a circle. Then I was in agony, for my left hand was covered with warts, and I was sure that whoever had to hold my hand would find it repulsive. At long last, I heard of a remedy for removing warts, and I lost no time in buying some nitric acid with which to burn them off. I applied the acid to two of my most gigantic warts and watched them turn black and begin to peel off in layers. By the time these two had burned down to the bottom and left scars behind them, the rest of the wart family had mysteriously disappeared without any medication.

Our folk dancing class rehearsed for a long time to do a number for some kind of festival in the Ojai Park. The festivities were at night, and I wore a costume that made me look like a poppy. The family was there to watch me go through my role.

Doris Cross was my bosom pal for a while. She and Charles Bogner had a crush on each other and she and I used to spend our recess periods in playing our own version of hide and seek with Charles B. and his chum. I was the go-between for Doris and Charles. He had forcefully taken her belt from her and when he returned it by me, he put a

miniature picture of himself under the elastic band that
went around the rolled-up belt.

In April of 1930, we moved to the front house on the lot on
Grand Avenue. There we had two bedrooms, a living room,
kitchen, screened porch and bath. Momma and Daddy no
longer slept together. She was by now bedridden
constantly. Daddy and I did all the cooking. He cooked
pork roasts (boiled them) which we had for Sunday
morning breakfasts and as long as it lasted thereafter. I
made the biscuit dough every evening before going to bed
and rolled it out and cut the biscuits so that they were ready
to put into the oven in the morning. Daddy usually washed
dishes and I dried them. We boiled the ones Momma had
used. I began cooking cereal for her breakfast.

I was doing all the housework that was done. Daddy
'bragged on me' to the Nortons and other people because I
was running the household practically, at the age of twelve.
I did the family washing every week in the machine,
carrying pans and buckets of boiling water from the stove
to where the machine set in the large bathroom. Momma
was always fearful that I would spill the boiling water on
myself, and she worried that I might catch my hands in the
wringer, as indeed I had caught my right forefinger one day
on Fulton Street.

On Mother's Day that year, we went to Sunday School, the
three of us. At the door, one of the church ladies stood,
giving out carnations to everyone…red ones for those
whose mothers lived and white ones to those whose
mothers were dead. She asked us, "You're the little Henry
girls, aren't you?" When we answered, "yes", she hesitated
just a moment before pinning red carnations on us. The
following year, if we had been there, we would have
received white ones.

I continued reading with an increasing fervor. I had read by now all the books that children read, those of Lewis Carroll, Mark Twain, the Oz books, the Campfire Girl series, the Elsie Dinsmore series, Edgar Allen Poe, ad infinitum. And I had gotten a little ahead of my age with the Gene Stratton Porter books and those of Edna Ferber, Kathleen Norris, Mary Roberts Reinhart, etc. Then I read a good many biographies and THE HISTORY OF MANKIND, by Henrik Willen Van Loon. I read thoroughly always and with deep concentration. A list that I kept of what I had read numbered over a hundred books to that time. I was so absorbed in my reading upon occasions that I allowed my culinary efforts to suffer. I let the beans burn more than once.

Another of my interests lay in masterpieces of painting. I had for some time been saving every reproduction that I could find in magazines and newspapers of the old masters…Millet, Rembrandt, da Vinci, Renoir, Bonheur, Reynolds, Gainsborough, Van Gogh, and on and on. I learned from my collecting that Jean Francois Millet used humble subjects, that his work was human and touching; Leonardo da Vinci specialized in Madonnas and sacred subjects; Jean Renoir painted a good many nude and half-nude portraits of his sweetheart and other women; Rosa Bonheur painted animals, horses and dogs; Vincent Van Gogh's brush betrayed his madness. One source of material for my collection was the Sunday school four-page leaflet. I enlarged my collection by seeking old discarded leaflets that had found their way into a dry creek bed that wound its way near our house. I picked them out from among other refuse, wiping the dog excrement off carefully when necessary.

The shingled hair cut was the fashion. Aunt Hattie tried to put me in style by cutting my hair, and in her attempt to get a gradual shingle up the back of my head she ended up by leaving practically no hair in the back. As usual after one amateur barber or another finished with my hair cutting, I was sick with disappointment and cried in anguish. I, who wanted above all else on earth to have a pretty hair do, was ruined. It was the wielding of the scissors by such unaccomplished and numerous persons that caused me to resolve that when I grew up I would never have my hair cut.

I was very unhappy with our home; it was so unattractive. I used to sit in the almost-unlived-in living room and plan where I would like to put a sofa, hang a picture, and set a lamp if ever the day came when there would be any money for such luxuries. Then I would be proud to invite friends to my house. Mrs. Fischer knew that I was ashamed of our abode, and she tried to encourage me by saying, "When the time comes that you're old enough to have boys come to visit you, you'll have a better and prettier home." She helped me to frame a picture which I hung in the living room. It was a scene of a peach orchard in bloom; I had torn it out of a magazine.

In this time, I was acutely and agonizingly aware of our poverty. The Bowies upon the hill sent large containers of wonderful home-made soup to us upon occasion. They would send it home with us when we were up there playing with Mary and Elizabeth. At Christmas, our other neighbor, Mrs. Smith (Rodney was a student at the exclusive boys' school) brought a large basket of brand new and exciting gifts to us. There were a book and a lovely doll with long blond hair that I treasured for years to come. For a while, we weren't sent to Sunday school because we couldn't go in the ragged shoes we wore to school. I was almost ill with compassion when I stood on the screened porch one early evening and watched Daddy as he stood in the yard between our house and Hagans.' He loved music, and the only way he could hear it was to listen surreptitiously to the Hagan's radio. If I felt any gratitude for anything, it was for the fact that the aged Hagans were hard of hearing and therefore had the radio playing loud enough so that Daddy could hear it too. Unobserved, as far as he knew, he stood with his head to one side, with a slight expression of pleasure on his face.

Kathryn Williams had asked me to go to a church program with her one evening. During the afternoon, I was wondering what I could wear and concluded that I would simply be unable to go. I told Momma that I *wished* I could just have a new pair of shoes, that I just couldn't go to the program in my worn, and reinforced-with-cardboard, shoes. When Daddy came home from work, Momma told him that I needed some new shoes, and to my infinite joy Daddy had enough money for me to get some. It was a new sensation I felt; the fact that I had expressed such an urgent desire for shoes made Momma determined that I should have them if possible. She knew that wouldn't have entered my head to ask for anything except a basic necessity. I felt that I was considered important enough to warrant this special sacrifice.

Recess was over and the bell rang to return to class, but I sat on the edge of the paved corridor outside the classroom with the worst headache I had ever experienced. The pain was at the base of the skull in the back; I was holding my head in both hands and crying. The teacher came out and said that I should go home. If she hadn't come out, I don't know what would have taken place. I wouldn't have gone home without being excused from school, and I wouldn't have walked into class and asked for an excuse. Maybe I would finally have been forced to go to Mrs. Sheldon's office and ask to go home.

Toward the end of the sixth year of school, I was among a few other students in winning a gold-colored medal with Thomas Edison's likeness on it as an award for having written an essay on his life. Graduation exercises for the class were held in the auditorium of the Nordhoff Union High School, where I would be attending Junior High the next term.

After school was out, we girls went to summer school. There I enjoyed working in handcraft for an hour or two at a time. I wove mats for hot plates out of string. And I worked for a long time on a bed jacket; it was made of pongee and lined with flannel, and I blocked a stylized flower design at the edges. It was to be for Momma. I didn't finish it in time.

Mr. Norton, for whom Daddy worked, gave him an old victrola with a good many used records. I was going to Sunday school again now with my new shoes, and when I came home every Sunday morning I found Daddy always sitting in the bare living room next to the victrola and listening intently to the assortment of records that included 'What a Funny Old World this World Will be in 1992' and 'Ragtime Temple Bells.'

Mr. Norton sent each of us children a dollar by Daddy one time. I accepted my dollar bill, caressed it, carefully straightened all the corners, examined it thoroughly for a while as I was dreaming of all the wonderful things I could buy with it. After I had called it my dollar for about an hour, I went to Daddy and gave it to him, saying that I knew he needed it more than I did. His financial status was such that he had to accept it. I certainly felt as much joy in giving it to him as I would have felt in spending it, a different medium of joy though it was. Daddy took it as a loan, the same as he had upon previous occasions of this type. From time to time, I used to add up in my mind all the money that I had given to Daddy after having received it as a gift. This last dollar brought the amount to seven dollars. I looked forward to spending this fortune someday when Daddy would be in a position to repay it. The time never arrived.

I was much too big for a tricycle by then, of course, but I had wanted one for so many years that I never admitted even to myself that I was now past the tricycle age. When I could wangle it, I took short rides on the little Donoghue girl's trike. My knees stuck out so far that it was difficult to peddle; the handlebars were in the way of my knees.

The County Health Department kept track of homes with persons with contagious diseases. Dr. King came to the house to look at Momma. There was nothing he could do, but he told her that the weight of a bag of sand on one portion of her chest would bring some relief. When Momma told me this, saying that maybe I could get a small bag of sand for her, I asked, "But, Momma, where would I get it?" She thought I might get it at school. There *were* a couple of sandboxes on the playground, but I couldn't visualize myself going there and getting it; there were always kids playing around on the rings and bars and swings. Anyone who might happen to see me would know that Momma was sick and that we couldn't afford any medical assistance for her...even if it would help. No, I didn't see how I could possibly go to the playground and get the sand. I left Momma's screened porch, having objected to the project, but never mentioning the reasons for my unwillingness to comply with her need. Several hours went by before I worked up the courage to get a paper bag out of the kitchen and start walking to the school grounds, as I had known all the time I would do. I told Momma that I was going somewhere else; I couldn't afford to make the statement that I was going to get some sand because then I would *have* to come back with it. This way, I would be able to look the situation over when I arrived there and if circumstances shouldn't prove favorable, I would have the opportunity of waiting until the following day to try again. However, as I walked resolutely toward the grounds, I determined that this would be the day. When I reached the sandbox, I took note of which kids were around. They all seemed to be younger than I was, so, steeling myself to be indifferent to any attention they might give to my task, I started to unfold my paper bag. But my eye was still peeled. Hurriedly, I refolded the bag and held it inconspicuously at one side, for coming along the rounds was one of my own classmates on a bicycle. I backed up against a nearby tree and leaned there with apparent nonchalance. After his departure from my sight, I set to work immediately. Without looking further, I opened my bag and began to fill it with double handsfull of sand as I squatted there. I worked feverishly, but I exercised care in getting the cleanest sand. As I rose from my haunches and held the sand in my hand, I encompassed the whole playground at a glance then started for home. As soon as my feet were on the street, I relaxed and began to feel good in my accomplishment. It was so wonderful to walk onto the screened porch and show Momma what I had done. She had undoubtedly known all the time what my course of action would be.

Daddy saw some cough medicine that was advertised and sent away for it for Momma. He must have known that it would be of no curative value, but maybe he was trying to give her some temporary relief. I was vaguely aware of mixed emotions when I saw the 'medicine;' they amounted to pity for both Momma and Daddy. Did he have in faith in this brown liquid's ability to help Momma? Did he expect her to think it might help? Or what kind of gesture was it?

I couldn't fully realize how irremediable Momma's condition was at that point, but when she talked about the things that all of us would do together 'when I get well,' I felt within me that it was only something pleasant to talk about, dream of. When she said, in answer to Virginia's and Grace's queries, that we would go here or there on a big picnic, it sounded lovely and warm. I summoned a mental picture of how we would all look on a sunny day, walking across a vast expanse of grass with our food containers in our arms, looking for the ideal spot for our picnic.

That summer, I cleared off a space of earth under the trees near our house. There I marked off the clearance into four tiny rooms and enjoyed the last playhouse I ever made. I didn't use the playhouse to mother a doll. I used it only as a retreat when I wanted to read or work on my 'famous pictures' collection. It was hidden in the underbrush so that I could read undisturbed for as long a time as I had before starting supper, and I relished the luxuriant sensation of being alone in my own domain.

I closed my eyes one night to go to sleep and there followed an inexpressible sensation, the like of which I had experienced only once or twice previously but have felt periodically since. As I lay on my back, in the darkened room, I felt myself beginning to recede into space. As a result of this floating back into nothingness, which was strangely lacking in motion, I felt myself grow smaller and smaller until at last I was no more than a pinpoint within abysmal space. I seemed, when I stopped receding, to be resting on a desert, so barren and so boundless that it was beyond conception. There was no horizon. I lay encompassed by limitless area. It was horrifying to feel so infinitesimal, and I opened my eyes wide. This did nothing to dispel my hallucination, and I called Momma, aware that she would have to struggle to get out of bed to come to me. When she reached my bed, I could find no words to describe what I had just felt; in fact, I was not yet completely back to earth. I simply said that I felt 'funny' and 'far away.' She told me that I had drunk too much milk just before going to bed and it had probably created gas, that I would be alright.

In subsequent occurrences of this nature, the sensation has sometimes been reversed. Instead of feeling a shrinking removal from things earthly, I have found myself growing larger and larger, becoming so immense that space has to expand to allow for my abstract growth. There is room for nothing except me within the confines of space. With my eyes wide open, I feel my limbs and pinch myself, trying to prove to myself that it is all visionary. But when my whole being is so enlarged, my hands in proportion to my limbs, the rubbing of my limbs does little to dispel the hallucination. There have been occasions when I experienced both the shrinking and growing feelings.

Mrs. Davis was a representative of the County Welfare and was sent to our house to arrange for us children to be farmed out to individual families or to be sent to an institution where our health could be protected and our living conditions improved. Daddy sat in our barren living room talking to her and refusing to allow us to be taken away from home.

We kids and Daddy were inordinately fond of apricots. When Mr. Norton gave us a lug of them from his fruit trees, the four of us sat and ate our way well through the lug.

Aunt Hattie was visiting us, and she and I walked over to see Mrs. Fischer. We found Mrs. F. in bed with her new baby, Emily, who had just been born that morning. It hadn't been time for her delivery, so Mrs. F. had thought she was suffering from an attack of indigestion. There had been no time to get her to the hospital in Ventura. Mr. Fischer and Paul had delivered the baby. We were surprised beyond words and were eager to get home and tell Momma. On the way home, I thought about the sense of some kind of gratification one feels when he is the bearer of such news, and I determined not to obey the usual impulse of children; I wouldn't run into the house ahead of Aunt Hattie and breathlessly tell Momma about the baby. I walked into the screened porch with Aunt Hattie and kept my mouth shut so that she could be the one to have the satisfaction of telling the news. She did it with, "Eliza, Mrs. Fischer has had her baby," then she went on to tell the details.

Daddy bought a used Model T Ford from Slim Fink (whom we sometimes called Flim Stink) for one hundred dollars, on terms. It was a little black coupe and certainly inadequate for the four of us…Momma wouldn't be able to go out in it. I found a little hand-carved and painted wooden dog behind the seat which I still have. That was the only automobile we ever owned.

I went to spend the night with Mrs. Fischer. It was a wonderful feeling to have a bedroom all to myself…not only a bed, but the whole room! And there was the additional pleasure of having a string hanging at the head of the bed so that I could extinguish the light *after* getting into bed. But with all these luxuries, I was so homesick that I almost died. I would have given anything to be squeezed into my own bed with Virginia and Grace. Mrs. Fischer asked if I was homesick and I said I wasn't at all. She said that if I was I shouldn't be ashamed to admit it and that she wouldn't have any respect for a little girl who didn't get homesick for her mother. When I made a comment about our using a different kind of soap from hers, which was Lifebouy, she remarked that any soap other than Lifebouy was inferior and that we should make it a point to get that brand. When I got up in the morning and made my bed before leaving the room, it was all in vain. She went into the room and pulled the covers back, opened the window wider and told me that a bed should be given a good airing every morning before making it up. I had acted under the assumption that I was getting an early start with the housework.

Virginia couldn't bear to be teased, and when Mr. Fischer jokingly called her a 'stick in the mud' she could hardly stand it. Then he enjoyed the joke all the more, of course.

When Virginia, Grace and I wanted to go to town one afternoon, Momma was asleep and we didn't dare awaken her to say we were going or to ask permission. We thought we figured out a terrific plan when we stood the broom between the mattress and the bedstead at the foot of the bed and pinned a note of our whereabouts to the broom straw. If Momma would wake up, she would see the note immediately and not worry about us. When we returned home, however, she scolded us and told us never to leave the house like that without telling her beforehand. Our reason for the trip to town was a One-Cent Sale that was on at Boardman's Drug Store. We fully expected to find all kinds of articles, including candy, on sale for one cent with no strings attached. It was a sad disappointment to be told that the only way we could purchase any of the on-sale items for a cent was to buy first the same item at the regular price. We couldn't help feeling that Mr. Boardman had been very foxy to use a ruse like that to lure us, all illusion, into the store.

In September, 1930, I started to Nordhoff Junior High School. After spending the first whole day in registering and locating my classrooms, I felt that I would enjoy this new school. But after I had attended it for two or three days, having been overwhelmed by the appearance of my History teacher (Miss Tomlinson, who wore a gorgeous pale green silk dress and who later created a scandal with Mr. Polski that caused his demotion from principal to teacher) I was informed that I would no longer be going to school. The health authorities had arranged for me to stay at home and keep up with my lessons with the guidance of a teacher who would come to the house for an hour each day. The schedule went into effect immediately and worked very well. I had time to do the housework, receive my hour's tutoring, do my homework and take an afternoon rest each day. The authorities had advised Momma to have us take a nap each afternoon for an hour, but we usually lay there restlessly until the hour passed. I liked my teacher, and she was pleased with my progress. We ordinarily sat on a bench that was built around the trunk of an oak tree in the side yard. Being outside for school afforded me a fine opportunity to wear my beautiful wide-brimmed yellow straw hat with the long brown grograin ribbon hanging in the back…my hat had belonged to a little rich girl before me. It had come from Mrs. Smith. Under these circumstances, with no classmates, I had no playmates. I didn't long for a playmate because I would have felt too ashamed to let anyone know why I didn't go to school. I still occupied all my spare time by reading.

As I sat in the Baptist Church, apparently listening to Rev. Whaley's sermon, I was thinking that I didn't possess exactly the right kind of faith…I couldn't feel it deeply enough to suit me. With my head lowered, I looked through a leaflet that I had just received in Sunday school class and my eye caught a question in bold-face type: "HOW CAN I FIND THE TRUE FAITH?" Sure that I would find my answer here, I started reading. This was almost like finding an answer to a prayer. I read every work, trying to absorb the conviction that I sought, but the writer's time was wasted as far as I was concerned. I felt no surge of understanding. The words were not convincing in the least. I was truly disappointed when I realized that the article in which I had placed my hope had failed. I could think of no other source that would offer me an answer.

In the middle of the night, I was awakened by Daddy's crying. He was walking back and forth from the screened porch to the kitchen in his BVD's and crying, "My sweet girl; oh, my poor darling." The kitchen light was on and I could see his distracted figure…walking, crying, holding his head. Terrified, I called to him, "Daddy." He came on into the bedroom, sobbing. "Your sweet Mother; I can't wake her up. She won't wake up." He had been roused from his listening sleep by Momma's terrible effort to breathe, to capture a little air for her almost completely destroyed lungs. In her unconscious struggle, she was heaving and moaning. Seeing Daddy so distraught, and knowing that something ungodly was happening to Momma, I went into a violent fit of sobbing and involuntary trembling.

Early the following morning, Mrs. Schute came to the door of the screened porch with a container of hot vegetable soup. Having heard Daddy's cries in the night, she said to Momma, "You must have had a bad night; didn't you?" Momma answered, "Yes, they tell me I did." She had felt 'something give' in her chest a day or so before when she was getting into bed again after having gone to the bathroom.

Aunt Hattie told Daddy that something had to be done to alleviate Momma's constipation. The other day when she had gone to the bathroom, she had 'lost at least a pint of blood.'

Some charitable woman who liked Momma came again and brought a large paper sack of okra. We girls didn't like the vegetable at all, and we wished with all our might that she'd stop bringing it, but it grew in profusion in her garden and it was good nourishing food. Besides, it was free.

On December 5, 1930, three days before my thirteenth birthday, an ambulance drove to the door of the screened porch. Two men in white came in and put Momma on a stretcher. We children walked down the steps after them and looked through the windows at Momma as she lay in the ambulance. The last thing she said to us, before the ambulance drove off, was, "You children be sure to wear your coats after I've left." Her eyes glistened as she spoke. The house seemed awfully strange and lonesome when we went back in. Somewhat silently, the three of us walked out again, wandered to town and back, passing the time until Daddy would be home from work.

Thereafter, Daddy went to visit Momma in the Ventura County Hospital on Sundays. Sometimes, we went along, but we weren't allowed to enter the hospital ward where Momma lay with a great many other tubercular patients. Daddy would go in and sit beside her bed and we would stand outside the window and smile through at her. She was glad that she had a bed on the south side of the ward because the sun shone through her window.

Aunt Hattie was at our house one day when a delegation of women came from the church to clean and disinfect our house. They were all ladies that I had seen many times at church, and I had gone to school with some of their children. But I deeply resented their presence in the capacity of house fumigators, in the name of charity. When I saw one of them insert some salve in her nostrils to prevent the breathing in of germs, I was mortified and detested the situation. I would have a hundred times rather have cleaned the closets myself. I asked Aunt Hattie, "Why do they have to come here?" She told me not to be 'skeptical' about people…and thus I learned a new word.

Mrs. Downey was paid by the County to spend her days at our house with us girls. She was an Ojai housewife who could use the few extra dollars, and she had no children of her own to busy her. She was a soft-spoken brown haired and dark eyed youngish woman whose slowness in movement must have been due to some glandular condition. We obeyed her, as Daddy had told us to do, and she never had occasion to raise her voice to us. She carried on the command to see that we had an hour's nap every afternoon. Instead of napping, though, I spent my hour in dreaming and praying that my dreams would be answered. In January we found that we were to be sent to a preventorium the following month. It was a place where there would be other children in our circumstances. So every afternoon, my hour passed about like this: "Oh, God," I prayed, "please let there be a boy who likes me, please let me have a room by myself, and please let there be a library. Thy will be done; but *please*, God."

Momma's birthday was January 30th, and Daddy was wondering what he could get for her. He and I stood in the kitchen. He was at the sink getting a drink of water, when he said, "I wish I knew what to get for your Mother. I'm afraid she won't have another birthday. She's been wanting a clock, but I don't know...."

~ Preventorium ~

The preventorium was a form of preventative care. As early as 1909 pre-tuberculosis children, which included children in a tuberculosis household, were institutionalized in order to receive rest, fresh air, a well-regulated regimen, and good nutrition.
- What Is a Preventorium? H. E. Kleinschmidt, MD -

Fillmore

Fillmore
February 1, 1931 – August 15, 1931
~Genevieve, 13 years old, Virginia 11, Grace, 8~

It was on Sunday, February 1, 1931, that we girls packed a few miserable belongings into corrugated boxes and put them into the old Ford. Then Daddy and the three of us squeezed onto the one seat and drove to Fillmore, about twenty-three miles from Ojai. Daddy referred again to the slip of paper that had the address of the preventorium written on it. Without much difficulty, we came to a stop in front of an old-fashioned white two-story house. On the lawn in front was a sign, PREVENTORIUM. It was a new word to us. Daddy had explained that it designated a place where people were prevented from getting t.b. As we opened the doors of the car, got out and straightened our crumpled dresses, the noses of a half dozen curious faces were pressed into the glass of the big front window of the house. We were expected; Mrs. Coach held the front screen door open for us as we walked toward her. I stared incredulously at the size of her while Daddy introduced himself and us. She was the fattest human being I had ever seen. Three layers of chin hung over the peter pan collar of her white nurse's uniform. Her eyes were almost hidden behind the mounds of flesh that were her cheeks, but they seemed to be pleasant eyes.

Here was a whole group (about fifteen) of underprivileged girls and boys; they were in no better circumstances than I was and only two of them were older than I was. I grasped the situation almost immediately, and feeling inferior to none of them, I fashioned a new personality for myself. As I stood before all of them that first day, I met their curious staring with my head up and an unfamiliar confidence in my returned gaze and in my bearing. It was a little labored and affected at first, I will admit, but as the days passed, and the months, it became a natural part of me. I became vivacious. As I descended the stairs one morning, laughing and joking, Mrs. Coach said to her assistant, "That girl has too much nervous energy and pep for her name. I think we'll call her Ginger hereafter. Yes, that's it; Ginger." She was smiling. I liked her, and I liked my new name.

Almost at once I could see that my prayers were being answered. I was given a room by myself in the 'little house,' there were a few shelves of books that might be called a library if I wanted to give God the benefit of the doubt, and lastly Mrs. Coach's young son was manifesting great interest in me.

The 'little house' was a small frame structure in the rear of the main building. It was partitioned off into two bedrooms and a school room. The small bedroom was given to me, and Virginia and Grace slept in beds that were at one end of the classroom. This dormitory was presided over by Mrs. Coach's assistant, Mrs. Henry. And she wasn't the only Henry besides us three. Her husband and son, also Henrys, lived in a house several blocks away. Besides them, next door to the preventorium lived another Henry family...man, wife and a daughter who was even named Genevieve. This daughter I had seen before when she lived in Ojai the first year we were there. Since she was a few years older than I, we never became well acquainted. And there was also a fellow inmate whose name was Angie Enriquez, which translated from the Spanish, means Henry. The tree outside my window in the 'little house' was home to a great many pigeons that roosted there. Their cooing became part of my life.

Life was strictly routine. At seven in the morning, everyone was awakened by a hand bell that Mrs. Coach rang. After we donned our sun suits, and washed our faces, we sat at a long table to breakfast. There was a lot of mush for the morning meal; and milk was delivered to the institution in huge galvanized containers…skimmed milk because that was a good way to save on the allowance for food. Two children at a time took turns drying the dishes for a week at a time, while Mrs. Henry washed them. At eight-thirty the school bell rang…this time it was a hand bell rung by Mrs. Hiller. The classroom was conducted exactly like a country school, where one teacher heads all classes. I learned parts of speech in English, transportation in History, etc. At nine-thirty, there was a recess when all of us lined up in the main building for taking of temperature and feeling of pulse. At ten-thirty, another recess when we were served a glass of skimmed milk with cookies. School was out at noon, and shortly thereafter we had lunch. Dishes again. A sunbath, an afternoon nap, temperature and pulse taking again, another snack, homework, dinner, dishes. After which we sat in the living room and listened to the radio, played Old Maid, etc., until about eight-thirty when we were shooed off to bed.

The sun-bath was some process. Large mats were carried into the back yard, one for girls and one for the boys. The boys lay first on their stomachs so that the girls could lie on their backs with the tops of their sun suits pulled down to the waist. The boys supposedly couldn't peek at us so easily if they were on their stomachs. After fifteen minutes in these positions, Mrs. C., who was sitting on the back steps to watch us, called time to turn over for the girls. As soon as we had adjusted our sun suit tops, the boys turned over.

On Sundays, the sun bath was omitted and we wore our own clothes all day. I had brought a few of my best dresses that Mrs. Smith and other charitable souls had seen fit to provide me. At this stage I refused to wear a dress that didn't have some kind of sleeves. Hair was growing under my arms and I felt that it was too unattractive to be seen. We had to be clean and brushed by ten in the morning on Sundays because at that time representatives arrived from the Four Square Gospel church to minister spiritual help to us. We sat in two rows of kitchen chairs and listened to our lesson and sang hymns. The Catholics weren't forced to join us; it was optional.

Sunday afternoons were for visitors, relatives and friends of the children. There were very few visitors indeed. Daddy came to see us, but he had to reserve part of his time for visiting Momma.

Someone furnished some Valentine cards for us to send out. We three girls picked the biggest and prettiest one we could find in the lot and wrote lovingly on it to Momma. We hadn't seen her since before coming to the preventorium. The day after Valentine's Day, the dining room was full of sun-suited kids when the telephone rang. Mrs. Coach answered it and after listening for a minute asked the party to hold on while she told us all to go out and play in the yard. There was a mass exit and nothing else was said about the telephone conversation. But Virginia, Grace and I were surprised a little while later when Daddy came in, for it wasn't Sunday. Mrs. C. saw that we were left alone in the dining room and Daddy sat down while we three stood around him, waiting. He embraced us together and his voice broke as he said, "My little girls, your sweet Mother passed away last night." The four of us simultaneously began crying…such an abysmal feeling of loss, such emptiness. We clung together, the remainder of a family. That was the 15th day of February, 1931.

Three days later, Daddy came to take us all to the funeral. We crowded into the car once more and took the silent and miserable drive back to Ojai. Daddy wondered if we should leave Momma's wedding ring on her finger and I said we should. In the little cemetery between Ojai and Meiners' Oaks, we watched Momma's coffin being lowered into the earth. Then Aunt Ivory drove us back to the preventorium. In her concern she made an effort to console us by telling us that Momma hadn't suffered at the end, that she had died in her sleep. (After years of inexpressible suffering, a quiet and unconscious ending. That didn't help a lot.) And now that she had been dead for three days, her soul had gone to heaven, Aunt Ivory said. A soul in heaven would be a beautiful thought if such a thought were credible. I wanted to believe it.

That evening after the funeral, we went to bed in the 'little house,' the three of us. Grace and Virginia called out frequently to see if I was asleep yet. I wasn't, so they asked occasionally, "Are you afraid?" To lend them courage, I kept denying that I was afraid. But the longer I lay there in the dark, the more frightened I became. I plainly saw ghosts and spirits floating in the darkness of the room. They were so vivid and so eerie that I finally had to drop my brave front. I called out to the kids that I was going to the main building to get Aunt Jessie (Mrs. Henry). Virginia said, "I thought you weren't afraid." Since I was scared to go from building to the other by myself and the kids were afraid to be left alone, we all three went into the other house. Aunt Jessie was annoyed that we wanted her to come out of bed so early, but finally said, "Well, if that's the way you're going to be..." and went back with us to the 'little house.'

Sundays after that, I was unable to sit through the singing of the hymns. I'd begin crying and leave the room.

One day, a school bus was sent to take everybody to the dentist at the Ventura County Hospital. There were so many of us to see that dentist that those of us who had to wait until the last were nervous wrecks by the time our turn came.

Jean Coach, Mrs. Coach's daughter, deeply resented having her home full of skinny waifs. She was going to Fillmore Junior High School and her social status was not enhanced, she figured, by her mother's occupation. Mrs. C. tried hard to make life to Jean's liking, and I always felt sorry for her when Jean rebuffed her motherly advances. She was a very ill-humored girl and preferred not to become friendly with us girls who were her age. I never blamed her at all for that attitude; it was obvious that she could choose friends on the outside who were in her class. I used to marvel at her red hair with its crisp waves. In the summertime, to cool off, she dunked her head almost daily in a pail of cold water, and I was amazed every time to see the waves snap back into her hair as it dried. She had a wonderful collection of movie stars' pictures which she sometimes condescended to let us look at.

A few of us older girls were taken to the high school auditorium to see a presentation of Joan d' Arc, which impressed me greatly.

Aunt Harriet, as I think I began calling her about that time, moved to Fillmore that year and we girls sometimes went over to visit her for an hour or so in the afternoon. There was a magazine at her house with a gorgeous cover picture of Ginger Rogers who was becoming very popular.

Pauline and Eugenia Hancock, whom we had known slightly in Ojai, arrived at the preventorium. Pauline and Mrs. C. never got along together very well and one day Mrs. C.grasped Pauline's waist-length pigtails and yanked them gustily because Pauline made some deprecating remark about the mercurochrome that was being used on an injury of hers. She wanted iodine. Both the Hancocks were very religious and Pauline taught me biblical verses. I memorized all of the books of the Bible with her coaching. I read the New Testament, every word. The two of them slept in the extra bedroom in the 'little house' with us. One night, I was horrified to see Eugenia walking in her sleep with her hair screwed up in rag curls all over her head and her wide white nightgown dragging the floor. She put on one of her shoes and was going through the motions of tying the laces with her foot up on the classroom bench. Pauline got her back to bed.

The odor of the sugar refinery permeated every nook and cranny of Fillmore, stronger at some times than others. That and the rich fragrance of narcissus that grew in the yard have stuck with me.

We were moved from the 'little house' to the main building where I shared a room with Pauline. One evening, just after I got into bed, Jack Coach and his cousin Jack Boothe who was visiting him clambered up to the second-story window of the room I was in and would have come into the room except for my remonstrations and Pauline's horror. Jack C. had a crush on me. I had worked to instill it in him and after I had succeeded, I was interested in spreading my charm elsewhere. I had picked then on his cousin Jack B.

And there was George Fowler who lived next door to the preventorium. He and I played the common touch-and-go games by flashlight with the other kids in the warm summer evenings.

I made a few garments for my blond doll to wear...the one Mrs. Smith had given me. I kept her wardrobe in a shoe box, and upon departing from the preventorium I forgot and left both the doll and her wardrobe in a little closet in my room. I wrote to Mrs. C. later and asked her to send it to me, but it never came.

It must have been from some kind of nervousness that my skin became maddenly dry. When I lay down in the afternoon for my nap, I frequently had to get up and go downstairs to the bathroom and sop water all over my legs. The skin felt so dry and brittle that it was unbearable. I was constantly sticking my hands under the faucet to keep them wet. When no faucet was available, I licked them.

Just before our arrival at the preventorium, Mrs. Coach had had some trouble with a few of the girls who slept in the 'little house.' It was discovered that boys were climbing over the board wall during the evenings to see the girls. Those particular girls were sent away. One summer day a group of us was playing in the front yard and Mrs. C. sat on the porch. An old jalopy that was overflowing with teenage boys drove up the street and upon seeing us in our sun suits several of them whistled, called and waved at us. Entirely unaware of the passing car, I was calling a neighborhood dog that we often played with. With my arm outstretched, I was saying, "Here, Bowser; here, Bowser." Mrs. C., with all the noise the children were making, didn't hear what I was saying but she saw my outstretched arm and assumed that I was waving at the boys. She called me sharply, and the tone of her voice silenced the others. Her sudden and unexpected harshness startled me and it was a moment before I realized what she was accusing me of. I tried to explain that I hadn't waved at anyone, that I was only calling Bowser, but in my sensitivity I broke into such wracking sobs that I couldn't even speak coherently. I gave up the attempt and ran into the house and up to my room, aching under the impact of the unjustified scolding.

One of our pastimes was in jumping off the slanting roof of the garage onto a mattress that lay on the ground. We all took turns in executing the jump.

Our favorite radio programs were those of Pauline Holden, Loyal Underwood and His Cowboys, and the like. And Kate Smith, with her theme song 'When the Moon Comes Over the Mountain.' Also popular were 'River St. Marie' and 'Yes, You, You're Driving Me Crazy.'

The whole institution was thrown into commotion one day when Mrs. Coach discovered that little Willie Baker had lice after he had done some complaining and considerable scratching. Upon examination, it was found that his brother and a few other children were also victims. Out came the clippers and off came the hair of all the boys. The girls were let by with Larkspur applications, except some of the very young ones whose hair was cropped to within an inch of their scalps. For, after a couple of days, we were all preyed upon by the lice. Still yearning for wavy hair, I came within a hair's breadth of having Mrs. C. clip my hair close to the scalp, for I had heard of cases where hair came back in curly. True the cases were the ones where the hair had first fallen out due to fever, as in Marcella Bogner's history.

One morning, the grounds were all wet from the previous night's rain. There was a new little patient with us who was only about five years old. She was so small and thin that I easily hoisted her upon my shoulders; I was giving her a piggy-back ride along the slippery cement walk beside the house, and when I lost my footing I fell flat on my stomach. I had my right arm outstretched in an effort to break the fall and when I went down my passenger lit on my right shoulder. That created a very painful sprain and when I got up my arm hung limply at my side. I felt so sickened by the pain that I was led upstairs to my bed, my face drained of color. Jack Coach was the first one to reach me when I cried out after falling, and it was he who supported me until I was on the bed...with several others following us. Even through the pain, I was aware of the sweet pleasure that Jack's tenderness created in me. After the others had left the room, he stood beside my bed, looking down at me solicitously. For days, my right arm was useless.

And I thought I was going to die one day when I became ill from eating a good many fresh apricots without washing them thoroughly beforehand. Mrs. C. nursed me until the poison was carried off...the spray that had been used on the fruit in the orchard.

Came a day when Mrs. C. announced that we were all to be sent elsewhere; the preventorium was being disbanded. That was very disconcerting news to me; I had come to feel a certain security under that roof. The other children all liked me and flattered me about my pretty profile, my legs, etc. Where else would I be so highly esteemed? I left my room during my afternoon rest period and went downstairs to cry on Mrs. Coach's ample bosom. I was afraid to go out into the world again, to mingle with the unkind public school students. Yoba and her sister, Marie, and Paula and the others didn't seem to be very concerned about leaving however. And Virginia and Grace anticipated something better than the institution.

Ventura

Ventura
August 15, 1931 – July 15, 1932
~Genevieve, 13½ years old, Virginia, 12, Grace 8~

It was on a Sunday again, August 15, 1931, when Daddy came in the old Ford to transport us and our corrugated boxes to Ventura. On the way, he told us about the 'nice couple' we were going to live with. We seemed to be living in a circle…Ventura, Ojai, Fillmore, now back to Ventura again. When Daddy told us the name of the people with whom we were going to stay, it was to us a new one … Kipling. We stopped in front of a good looking home on Dunning Street, certainly more attractive than any house we had ever lived in.

Mrs. Kipling was a woman somewhere in her fifties. Her white hair was somewhat yellowed from the curling iron she used. That first day she was wearing a two-toned lavender knit suit which fit snugly over her firmly corseted matronly figure. Her lipstick ran into the wrinkles emanating from her lips and her face powder was too light for her darker skin. Mr. Kipling was a man of about her age whose face was marred by a jagged scar that wound its torturous way down his right cheek and over that corner of his mouth. They were both very pleasant; her attitude was affected and somewhat forced, but his was genuine.

Shortly after Daddy left us, Mrs. K. served an early Sunday dinner in the dining room. The main dish was stew and it was an appetizing one, but Grace didn't much like stew. Besides that, she was a little ill at ease, and she started complaining of being sick at her stomach. Mrs. K. didn't believe she was sick (and, indeed, I learned later that she was right) and didn't want her to leave the table. But I spoke up and said that Grace really was sick; otherwise, she wouldn't say she was. At last, she was permitted to leave the table and go to the bedroom that had been assigned to her and Virginia.

We were soon calling the Kiplings Aunt Margaret and Uncle George at their suggestion. I instituted a habit that annoyed both Virginia and Grace, namely that of kissing Aunt Margaret goodbye when we left the house for any length of time. I suppose I was that hard-up in my desire for intimacy and affection.

I had an attractive and spacious room of my own. Since I was told not to mar the walls by nailing up pictures, I used tape to stick up photographs of Sue Carol and Nancy Carroll.

In the early part of September, Mr. and Mrs. K. drove me to Ventura Junior High School to register for the eighth grade. The school was so comparatively immense and so spread out that I was awfully confused, but while they waited for me in the car I went about getting myself enrolled. They had given me a dollar for my student body card. I was directed to a desk that was set in the corridor where I would apply for my program. There was a long line. I had not the slightest idea what a program was for, so I asked if it would be necessary. I was told very brusquely that, "Of course you have to have a program. You can't go to school without one." A woman furnished it for me and I discovered that it was a schedule of classes that I would attend. This woman turned out to be a home economics teacher and I was in her class when school started the following day or so…Miss Sugars.

Miss Sugars was a terror and all kinds of stories went around among the students of how she had thrown pans at unruly pupils in her cooking class. I did fine in her class though since I never was aggressive enough to irritate her. She gave me an A for my cook book, which was in reality a composition book wherein I had entered the necessary recipes that we used in cooking. She also gave me first prize of one dollar for a book that I put together, one which told a story in pictures with subheads written beneath them. I spent long hours in perusing magazines to find suitable pictures to present my story and to keep the main characters in character. That project was for 'home room' over which Miss S. presided. In that room, she talked to me alone one day and told me that I should definitely plan to go to college, that if I couldn't afford it that I should work toward a scholarship.

My music appreciation class was one of my favorites. Miss Paddock with the receding chin was the teacher. In this class, we were rehearsed in a musical presentation which we gave for the whole school. I played the part of an old woman and had to flour my hair thoroughly to have it in keeping with my role. It was a slight part but it was still a feat to stand up and open my mouth before over a thousand people. I wanted badly to learn to read music and I was bewildered by the fact that our music books had all oval notes. How could a person ever learn which was which? In North Carolina our notes had been of various shapes and that would have been easier to comprehend. Miss Paddock explained that one note could be distinguished from another by the position it occupied on the scored lines, but it wasn't the function of that class evidently to learn to read music. The primary object was to learn to appreciate what we heard in music. And I did. I thoroughly enjoyed the recordings of Erlking, Marche Slav and all the others. I can still hear the touching cries of the little boy as he was borne through the forest on a racing horse, held in the arms of someone who was apparently Death. "Father, my Father," he wailed…that was the Erlking. At that time, I read the autobiography of Madame Schumann-Hinck. Because of my good grades in this class, I was chosen, along with another girl, to accompany Miss Paddock to a harpist's recital in town. It was the first harp I had ever seen and I was entranced.

Walter Gregg and Granville Lambert were both in that class and at various times I had crushes on them.

I spent some of my Saturdays' spare time in drawing marigolds and castor beans in the back yard. They were good too; the drawings, that is. I also drew small portraits of Grace and Mrs. K.

Not all was sweet and lightness around Mrs. Kipling. She had the well-known Irish temperament. Aside from that, there wasn't much love between her and us and she was easily irritated by us. She and I had a lively quarrel one day over what I would take to school in my lunch. She called me a couple of names, not obscene ones but uncomplimentary. I called her 'crazy' and threatened to tell Daddy on her. When he arrived the next time, I did mention it. She and he went at it for a while about the fact that we girls were not gaining weight to satisfy Daddy.

Virginia and Grace were attending Mound Grammar School. I went there one evening to see a program that they both appeared in. I felt like a grown-up, coming to see my little sisters perform at the grammar school.

I began suffering unexplainable attacks of dizziness. Any time that I would get up after having been lying on the bed, everything would go black and I'd start reeling. Mrs. Kipling, who had inquired among her friends and obtained some cast-off clothes for us, had difficulty in getting me to stand for fittings preparatory to altering them. I wasn't steady enough to stand still. When returning from an American Legion meeting one evening where we had accompanied the Kiplings (Mr. K was a veteran of the World War; that's where he had acquired his scarred cheek), my drawers became spotted. I showed the stains to Mrs. K., but she gave me no clear idea of what was going on. This happened several times and I was terribly apprehensive, knowing that it was leading up to something, but not knowing exactly how or when the climax would come. I was very uninformed and couldn't bring myself to ask anybody what I should expect. At last, three days before my fourteenth birthday, I 'became a woman.' I couldn't eat breakfast that morning. Mrs. K., with a knowing smirk on her face, said, "You don't feel very well, do you?" It sounded exactly as if she had said, "See, that's what you get; it serves you right. It isn't very pleasant, is it?" Instead of suggesting that I stay home that day, she gave me a gigantic folded square of old sheeting to put on and sent me off to school where I squirmed in misery the whole day. I was afraid to sit because I was sure I would get up and find spots on the back of my dress. I dreaded walking because the sheeting felt so insecure and uncomfortable. I moved around with my legs closed together.

I spent many an hour on my knees of the low window of my room. Before going to bed, I knelt there…thinking, dreaming, watching the stars, praying and inhaling the fragrance of the night flowers that bloomed outside the window.

The Kiplings had some friends in San Diego named Sweeney…more Irishmen. Aunt Sadie and Uncle Jack Sweeney, as we came to call them, visited in Ventura every now and then, and we went to San Diego to see them upon numerous occasions. We always enjoyed these trips immensely, usually stopping on the way to eat a meal that we had brought, on the beach. One evening, we left Ventura on the spur of the moment at about sundown. It was quite late when we reached San Diego. On the way, we made a discovery...Mrs. Kipling smoked. We had suspected it for some time, due to the finding of short cigarette butts with bobby pins that had acted as holders in the living room. We kids sat in the back seat and we saw the glowing end of a cigarette that Mrs. K. held as she snuggled close to Mr. K. in the front seat. We teased her about having finally been caught in the act, and though she was a little perturbed she couldn't do anything about it now. She used the bobby pins to keep from getting her fingers stained.

I think it was Roberta Barr with whom I went to see 'The Desert Song' on the stage of the high school one evening. It was very impressive.

I managed to make a few friends at school, but it was difficult because of the old inferiority complex that cropped out as soon as I got among people again (after the cloistered life of the preventorium). And now I was somewhat prudish, refusing to listen to dirty jokes and taking offense at people who used off-color language. Maybe I assumed the cloak of righteousness to avenge myself upon unfriendly people, or maybe I took it up as a way to justify myself for not making friends. It must have been some measure of compensation. Of the friends I had in school there...Arlene Hall, Marion Brown and Erna Dalheim...no one ever came to my house. I never invited them, for I knew they wouldn't have been welcomed with open arms. Arlene I had known in Ventura Avenue Grammar School, and Marlene I had known at Nordhoff Grammar. Erna was the only new addition and she was most to my liking, but I even refused to listen to her off color girlish jokes. She laughed at me for it.

Back in Ventura, letters began arriving from Jack Reich. The first one was addressed to me on Dening, Derning and finally Dunning Street, with the first two spellings crossed out.

On July 4th, Uncle George Kipling gave us kids a dollar to divide between us. He did it on the sly and bade us keep it a secret. We said we wouldn't say a word about it to Aunt Margaret. Upon a couple of similar occasions in the past, he had given us similar amounts, unbeknownst to his spouse. But this time I was indiscreet enough to enter the item in my diary, a composition book that I left lying in plain view in my room…never giving a thought to the possibility of Aunt Margaret's being curious enough to turn its pages. The next day, she confronted us with the knowledge of our secret. She said she had seen in my diary that I was under the impression that Uncle George had given us the dollar of his own accord. But in reality, she said, she and he had talked it over in advance and had agreed upon the giving of it; she, indeed, had been the one to give him the idea. For Uncle George's sake, we fell right in with her lie and thanked her for the dollar. We knew that she had probably bawled him out in a rage after she had read my diary, and I felt miserable at having inadvertently betrayed his generosity.

The Kiplings began talking about the fact that they were going to sell their home and move up north. It was at first mentioned somewhat carelessly in our presence; before long a definite date was set for their moving, and we were informed (regretfully, of course) that they would have to let us be sent elsewhere. I enjoyed the prospect of the new surroundings, but I resented the fact that we were moved around, like so many inanimate checkers, at other people's whimsical notions.

Meiners'
Oaks

Meiners' Oaks (pr: Miners)
July 15, 1932 – June 26, 1935
~Genevieve 14½ years old, Virginia, 13, Grace, 9~

Once again the old Ford and the corrugated boxes came
into play. We bade the Kiplings goodbye on their front
lawn. Resentment rankled within me, and I said goodbye
and thanks without kissing them. Virginia and Grace
followed my suit. Even though I hadn't openly doubted the
fact that they planned to sell their house, I knew within me
that it was their way of ousting us without having to resort
to the brutal truth…it was a ruse. I was glad of one
thing…that I wasn't having to change schools in the middle
of a term. It was the 15th day of July, eleven months to the
day since we had entered their house. The wheel had not
yet ground to a stop; it was overlapping the circle and
turning us back to Ojai again. Actually, it was to Meiners'
Oaks this time…two miles west of Ojai…that we went. As
we stopped in the dusty driveway at Grayhaven, Miss Otis
came eagerly to the gate to meet us. She was a little bird-
like woman, slight and lively, and she extended herself
wholeheartedly to us at once. Following her, came Mrs.
Gray (whose home Grayhaven was) and Miss Bates. Mrs.
Gray was lacking in the motherly quality that Miss Otis
exuded, but she was pleasant. There were several bristly
hairs sprouting from her chin. Miss Bates was wearing a
hairnet that proved to be almost part of her dress. She was a
little hefty and on the jolly side.

Three childless women (Mrs. Gray a widow and Misses
Otis and Bates spinsters) and three motherless girls. At the
suggestion of one of them, we drew straws to pair ourselves
off. Grace drew Aunt Nellie, Virginia drew Aunt Lil, and I
drew Aunt Jeanette…Miss Otis, Miss Bates, and Mrs. Gray
respectively. In the pairing process, the types seemed to be

very well matched. As the time passed though, we kids became more and more aware that it was Aunt Nellie to whom we all belonged. It was she who championed us in every difficulty. When Miss Bates became irritated at our making unnecessary but to-be-expected-of-kids noise during the evenings when she wanted to hear the radio, it was Aunt Nellie who smoothed over the situation. When I spilled ink on the floor and Mrs. Gray was perturbed at the stain, it was Aunt Nellie who worked to help me remove the traces. At Christmas time, it was Aunt Nellie who helped us pack gift boxes of candied citrus peelings to send to our relatives. Of course, she was the one who had ordered us kids from the County in the first place; it just happened that she was living in Mrs. Gray's house. And, being the courageous and generous woman that she was, she did everything in her power to give us a genuine homely atmosphere. She sewed and worked for us beyond the call of duty, in return for the inadequate sum of twenty-five dollars a month she received for keeping each of us. The previous others had taken care of our physical needs, true; but Aunt Nellie added the warm and motherly touch that it isn't within everyone's power to give.

I spent some time in drawing. I sat for hours beside the passing road and drew Grayhaven, with its surrounding shrubs and flowers. I drew animals and a nude or two.

Through some source, we heard that Mrs. Coach had died of a heart attack. Though we had lived in her institution for a good many months, we had never come to know her closely, so we weren't much affected by the news. Virginia recalled the time that Mrs. C. had slapped her face for some small infraction.

In September, 1932, I went into the ninth grade in Nordhoff Union High School, the same school where I had started the seventh grade two years previously. There I saw Kathryn Williams again, for the first time in over two years. She seemed to have forgotten me entirely; therefore, I made no sign that I recognized her. She had changed a great deal. Her hair was now long and henna-ed. I found that she had no friendship with any of her classmates and that she went around exclusively with an older and faster group of girls and fellows from Ventura.

When Daddy came to visit us, I saw each time with renewed concern that he was ill. His coughing was more severe and he looked bad. I began praying each night before falling asleep that he wouldn't die too. Aunt Nellie, seeing me wandering around in a melancholy state one day, said that I should perk up, that 'the whole world should look rosy' to me at my age.

It was arranged for us to go to the Baptist Sunday school with Earl Taylor (whom I had last seen in 1928) and his sister Lois. He drove a red Durante convertible coup. With five of us in the car, two of us had to sit in the rumble seat. He was a competent driver, but with the zest of youth he took all kinds of chances and kept us scared half to death. It was always with nervous apprehension that we got into his car, and we used this fact to try to persuade Aunt Nellie not to insist that we go, but to no avail. I suppose she theorized that since we were on a worthy ride the Lord would see us safely to and from Sunday school.

One day we encountered a girl we had known at the preventorium. She was living with a family in town, but was too ill to attend school. Within a year, she died of tuburculosis.

I was still fourteen when I had my first bona fide date. There was a boy named Sherwood 'Bud' Trevor at school who was a grade ahead of me. I was kidded a lot about him because he had an obvious crush on me. I treated him politely but didn't in the least reciprocate his feeling toward me. I wouldn't have minded being kidded if he had been a more likely prospect, but he was a rather retiring boy who was lacking in popularity and I knew he was no 'catch' according to the popular conception of the word. When he asked me if I would go out with him, I thought, "why not?" Aunt Nellie consented, and she helped me get dressed. He drove up in an antiquated high sedan and came into the house. He got off to a good start with Aunt Nellie who had no use for a boy who would sit outside and honk the horn for a girl. I donned my beige velvet coat with the neck ties which were trimmed in fur (Aunt Nellie had requisitioned cast-offs for us from her friends, as had Mrs. Kipling) and Bud and I went to Ventura for a movie. I was home by eleven o'clock according to Aunt Nellie's stipulated time limit, having had a very uneventful and unstirring first date. The next day at school, the teasing was intensified, and I realized that for the sake of my reputation I would have to try to arouse the interest of a more desirable fellow.

Much to our chagrin, Aunt Nellie recruited another waif, a girl named Dorothy Lindsey. We objected aloud, but it might have been easier for Aunt Nellie to make ends meet if this project were run on a larger scale. We felt that it would greatly lower our prestige, not that we would get less attention from Aunt Nellie, but that the kids at school might become more consciously aware of the fact that we weren't boarding with an Aunt at all but that we were merely wards of the County. It was difficult to have to introduce Dorothy around and let it be known that she was a new addition to our house hold. But she was a year older than I was and older fellows came into my sphere through her. I went out once or twice with Earl Taylor when she was with Lloyd

Hayes. That way, I got closer to Lloyd's brother Jimmy, whom I doted on for some time.

During the summer of 1933, Aunt Nellie moved with her brood of four to 133 Lomita Drive in the Oaks. I started the tenth grade in September, 1933. That year, I was able to include orchestra in my curriculum, and Mr. Frank Roller, the music director had a beginner on his hands who was intent upon learning to master the most difficult of instruments. I studied and practiced with concentration. I never missed an evening practice hour in the old building. Since Lois Taylor also attended these practice periods, I rode with her and her father who drove us. For three years, I labored with the violin, and thoroughly enjoyed trying. But after the first two years, I reluctantly admitted to myself that I was working toward something I could never attain. Something was lacking; the only two requisites I possessed were an intense desire to learn the instrument and a willingness to work toward that end, but the necessary competency and personal tuterage was missing, as was the most important factor of all…innate aptness. I was always and inevitably required to play second violin, but I was still proud to be seen carrying the encased instrument to and fro.

In order to keep us and our cohorts entertained in the home, Aunt Nellie instituted the weekly congregation of several of my friends at our house. Lois and Earl Taylor, Anna Lee Byles and several others came over on Wednesday evenings. Earl or Anna Lee would play the piano, while the rest of us sang popular songs from the sheet music Aunt Nellie furnished. We sang songs like 'By the Waterfall' and 'I'll String Along With You.' Afterward, Aunt Nellie always served appetizing refreshments.

On February 4, 1934, Daddy sat in front of the fireplace with us and told us that he was going to the County Hospital. He coughed as he spoke, the old familiar cough of Momma's. We had never heard of anyone being discharged alive from that hospital, and it hurt to think of Daddy's taking a step of such finality.

I began to realize how absolutely alone I was; that is, it was a sensation that I became aware of, and I didn't know whether everybody else in the world felt the same as I did or whether they were able to share their innermost emotions with each other. One evening, I stopped, almost aghast, when I became aware of the sunset as I walked down an open road where the oaks didn't obscure my view. I watched the process as one hue blended with another and created a third. It was too beautiful. There was an aching that enveloped me as I thrilled to the marvel. What inspiration! The thing I wanted most on earth was to share the joy with someone, and it was so painful to realize that there was not a soul whom I could meet on this emotional level. The realization was unbearably depressing.

Aunt Nellie was the best substitute for a mother that could be found. I had resigned myself to wearing cast-off clothing. I had no shortage of boyfriends. I was popular and received good grades in school. There were moments when I thought I would burst with elation when there was no apparent stimulus. I would soar about freely with no motivation whatsoever except a thought or a dream that had suddenly come over the horizon of my mind. It was so wonderful to be sixteen! I thought with dread of the time when I would be a year older…two years older, five years. To be sixteen forever! It wouldn't be possible to have as much fun a short time from now as I was having at present. There would be new troubles to become reconciled to, new hurdles to jump, new obstacles on the course. I cut out a poem in a magazine that expressed it the way I felt and kept it. To be Sixteen! There were the little daily upsets, yes, and the problems that go with being sixteen. Daddy was in the County Hospital, and I never forgot that for long at a time. But the most oppressing worry I had was the constant one of being a ward of the County. If I shoved it, in its active state, out of my conscious mind, it retired to my subconscious were it worked assiduously to keep a gray veil drawn over the lustrous face of happiness.

Daddy visited us one day when one of the hospital nurses came to Meiners' Oaks and brought him to us. He was very weak and spent the afternoon on a cot in the yard. The sun and the air were pleasant to him. We had visited him infrequently in the hospital. We had been taken to see him once by Tommy and Frances Dills, and on the way home we had been frightened almost to death by Tommy's drunken driving. Poor Frances was almost in tears, as were the three of us. Frances knew nothing about driving, and she begged me to take the wheel even though I knew little more than nothing about driving. All I would have known how to do was to keep the car on the right side of the road, and that was more than Tommy was doing. When we were let out at home, still alive, we went into the house cussing, 'that damned fool, Tommy.'

One Sunday morning, June 9, 1935, Miss Bates came and told us that she had just had a phone call from the hospital. Since we had no phone, the hospital had been given Mrs. Gray's and Miss Bates' number. Daddy had suffered a hemmorage early that morning. She would drive us to the hospital to see him. Full of almost unbearable apprehension, we got ready and rode silently to Ventura. Aunt Nellie went into the hospital with us and waited while we visited with Daddy. He was almost in the company of death by then, but he smiled and tried to talk to us… "My little girls," he called us. His hair was uncombed. It was so difficult to keep my eyes on his face, but when they strayed it was even more ghastly to look at the blood-stained sheets and bedding rumpled around and over his emaciated body. Blood…on his bearded chin, and even on some of the bedside table objects. That was the last time we ever spoke to him. Aunt Nellie tried to console us.

Two weeks passed before Miss Bates came to tell us of the final phone call. Aunt Nellie cried with us, while talking gently. I clung to the hanging curtain that concealed our clothes closet and wept inconsolably. That was Sunday, June 23, 1935. Later in the day, Aunt Ivory came to see us. She and Uncle Lee had obtained Daddy's personal effects from the hospital, among which was the key to his trunk. Aunt Ivory wanted to know where the trunk was so that she could get a suit out of it for Daddy's burial, and she wanted to know which suit we wanted him to wear. I felt hesitant about allowing her to open the trunk and rummage through it, and when Aunt Nellie was able to get me alone she said that she agreed with me. Daddy's possessions, however miserable they were, belonged exclusively to us. So, Aunt Ivory suggested that I go home with her and spend the night and she would drive me to where the trunk was stored the following day. I didn't want to go away from home overnight, but it was necessary. I spent a lonely night in the bed of relations toward whom I felt little affinity. When I awakened in the morning, Monday, the radio was blasting out loud music. We drove up Ventura Avenue to the small business establishment of one of Daddy's friends, where his trunk was stored in a dusty corner. And there was the ancient leather armchair that Daddy had bought when we lived on Grand Avenue. I recognized it but my claim to it was disputed by the woman who had admitted us. She declared that she had bought it from Daddy some time ago. So the trunk was the only earthly possession Daddy had left. We extracted a dark suit from the bottom of the trunk and Aunt Ivory freshened it up at home. Then we drove to the mortuary with it. There, she waited for me while I went into the cubicle where Daddy lay. The mortician drew the somber curtains and I was alone with Daddy. I sat and studied him; then went to his side and for a moment I held his right hand that lay cold and rigidly on his abdomen. His face was now smoothly shaven and his hair combed. No more blood, just lifelessness. I was driven home that afternoon; there I wrote a letter to Rev. Whaley, asking him to officiate at Daddy's funeral. He was the Baptist preacher who had conducted Momma's funeral services.

The following day, Tuesday, Aunt Nellie and I went to Ventura again to arrange final details. I requested that the funeral be held as soon as possible. The man to whom we gave the vital statistics asked for details that would be printed in the newspaper. I asked him not to name the cause of Daddy's death, and I declined to give him our names as the bereaved. I also told him not to state the time that was arranged for the funeral services. I didn't want anyone to know anything. I refused to have public notice taken of the humiliating facts. I didn't want our names linked with the demise of a tubercular patient in the poverty-ridden County Hospital, and I didn't want anyone, friend or otherwise, to be at the funeral to witness our wretchedness.

Services were held during the afternoon, Wednesday, June 26, 1935, the day after Virginia's birthday. Aunt Nellie had arranged for Mrs. Humphrey to drive us to the little cemetery about a mile away. I hated the idea of having her take part in the whole proceeding; but there was no one else whom I would have appreciated in that role either. When I voiced my resentment to Aunt Nellie, she understood. Mrs. Humphrey wouldn't intrude, she said, and she had been kind to offer this needed service. There were no preliminary church services; Rev. Whaley simply spoke briefly at the head of the open grave, adjacent to the one where Momma lay. The casket wasn't opened. I had expected to have this last sight of Daddy, and I regretted that I hadn't gone in to see him the second time on the day that I had been in Ventura with Aunt Nellie. After the unbearably painful process of watching the lowering of the coffin, and after receiving the offered consolation, Mrs. Humphrey, who had waited unobtrusively for us, near her car, drove us home in our utter dejection. At home, Aunt Nellie served us some hot soup. I had no sooner gotten it down than I had to retire to the bathroom where my knotty stomach rejected it.

finis

Henry Girls' Graduation Pictures

Genevieve

Virginia

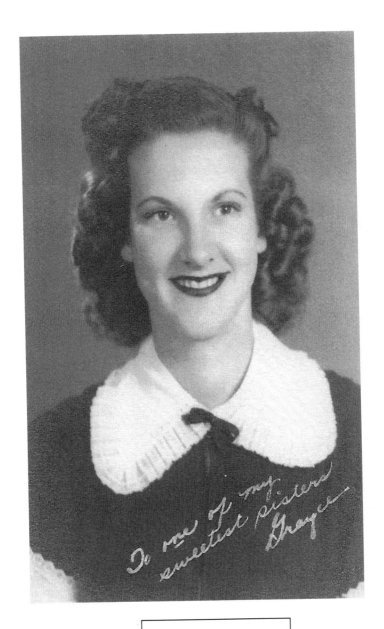

To one of my
sweetest sisters
Grayce

Grace

Afterword

Genevieve had become Ginger, Virginia became Virgi, and Grace changed the spelling of her name to Grayce. Grayce was my mom.

The girls' story is lined with hardship, family loyalty, and grit, which I believe was their legacy from Lewis and Eliza: just keep on going, and keep going together.

I knew each of the Henry girls through their adulthood, though distance separated us, and until their deaths. Each of them maintained kindness and good humor. They were able to give and receive love. And they were devoted to each other.

They married men who loved them and treated them well. Life dealt each of them some blows, as life is wont to do, but Ginger, Virgi and Grayce weathered it all with gracefulness and decency, and kept going strong to the end.

How they began and how they fared –

Lewis Cleveland Henry married Eliza Jane Peek in July, 1916. He was 30 and she was 24. Genevieve was born a year and a half later. The Henry and Peek families worked the farms and fields of the small town of Ellijay, North Carolina. Lewis and Eliza had each grown up with 10 brothers and sisters. Eliza was the first born in her family; Lewis was third born in his family.

The three little girls in our story were born in Ellijay. When they left for California, Genevieve was 9 years old, Virginia was 7, and Grace was 4. Genevieve would have probably known, her great grandparents, grandparents, and many of her aunts and uncles and cousins. Farms butted each other and families gathered together to plow and plant, and to bring in the crops and share in the bounty. As they were able, they would have assembled for hardships, for festivities, and for big decision-making sessions. Those who secured jobs in town would have made the effort to travel home over the years for at least some of the family tragedies, traditions, and reunions.

How Lewis must have struggled making the decision to leave the family support system, but it was based on the hope of Eliza's delicate health being restored. I am not sure at what age Eliza contracted tuberculosis, but Ginger told my mother, Grayce, that after she was born Eliza did not hold her for fear of spreading the dread disease to her youngest child.

The distance from Ellijay, North Carolina, to Ventura, California, is a straight horizontal line across the Google map, 2,277.2 miles. The family made the five-day journey by train in 1927. Lewis's older brother, Lee, and his wife, Ivory, had preceded them out west. Lee met them at the station and supported them for almost three weeks until they could move into their own place.

Once they arrived in California, the Henry's moved often, within a 20 mile radius. My count revealed that Aunt Ginger lived in 13 homes in her first 17 years.

Aunt Ginger does not mention the Great Depression of the 30s from her perspective in 1946, but surely Lewis's efforts at finding and keeping a job in order support his family were seriously affected by the nation's economy.

Lewis was a country boy from the back woods of the Smokey Mountains. To Californians, he sounded odd with his thick southern drawl. He was not a skilled laborer, and he was in and out of work. He had been a farmer, from a long line of farmers. Besides those agrarian skills he could probably also do carpentry and work with animals, perhaps blacksmithing. But town jobs were scarce, paychecks were unreliable, and their cupboards were often completely empty. The generosity of neighbors, even those who were pious or unintentionally inconsiderate, was literally life saving for the family. I thank God, even as I write this, for the hospitality the Henrys received. My mom and her sisters are some of the most precious people my sisters and I have ever known. I wish I could go back in time to embrace the people who were kind and long suffering toward them, sharing food and clothing, toys and household items.

When Eliza died in 1931, her girls were 13, 11, and 8. Lewis reluctantly received the help of the county and tried bravely to keep his girls with him. But he was forced to be practical because he knew he could not keep food on the table. Perhaps by then he was showing early signs of TB and that prodded him into making the decision for the girls to move into the preventorium. In my mother's family history, she writes that it was called The Preventorium Farm. I'm guessing Aunt Ginger must have recoiled from calling it that, even as an adult. The name would have been so degrading: one associates animals with a farm, not little children whose parent is sick and near death. What a stigma to deal with as a teen, or at any age.

Yet, life in the 1930's was unsophisticated and elected officials and their staffs had only so much financial capital to work with. Compassion and empathy would have been stretched thin in public service during those hard times. Not everyone had a telephone or a vehicle, people were pecking away on Remington typewriters or handwriting their notes and reports—the system was ponderous and slow moving.

And what about the three girls in foster care, and then orphaned when their father died? Their parents' next of kin, Uncle Lee and Aunt Harriet, lived in the immediate vicinity. Were they and the family members in North Carolina sought and questioned about providing a refuge for the orphaned girls? These are queries that were never answered. We do know that it was ideal that they lived in the foster home with Aunt Nellie. She was a kind, sensitive, and motherly woman that they praised in their adulthood. They were with her for four years. I'm sure that she scrimped and saved so that Genevieve and Virginia were able to have special dresses and professional graduation photographs. By the time Grace graduated, she lived in another foster home.

Genevieve's and Virginia's and Grace's earliest years were in the core of extended family in Ellijay. It was a very large extended family. And that is what Ginger, Virgi, and Grayce grappled with all of their lives, wondering: why didn't our relatives want us? Why didn't someone come and get us after our parents died? Were they afraid they and their children would also become sick? Were they so poor that they could not bring in other mouths to feed? But, we were f-a-m-i-l-y!

I know this question bothered each one, because I heard it quietly voiced at times over the years. Yes, there must have been a sour, bitter place in each of their hearts toward the relatives who ignored them, but primarily, I think, what each one harbored was the sadness of *'what was wrong with me that I wasn't wanted by any of them?'* And they must have questioned, *'Where were You, God? My prayers were not answered and my parents died.'*

These questions were never brought up for discussion in our family gatherings. The girls became women and the women did not want to discuss it. We respected their privacy and accepted the tidbits of information they shared with us.

Every one of us deals with insecurities and unanswered questions. For some it is crippling, and life is lived in a cage of sadness. These girls broke through the bars that could have confined them and set themselves to stay closely connected with each other and to stay engaged with everyday life.

If they had not become strong independent women, perhaps some judgment and blame would be lurking on the fringes and between the words of this story. But there is none. Explanations were never given by the southern relatives, and fences were mended years later. The Henry girls' story holds years of 'mostly' happily ever after.

The girls had survived a difficult childhood together, and their bonding was strong and unwavering. When Ginger moved away to Los Angeles after high school, Virgi and Grayce continued in foster homes until each one turned 18 and was emancipated from the system.

What happened next in the story?
After my husband, Dan, read *Remembering Genevieve*, he said that the reader will want to know…***what happened to her? how did her life go? what about her sisters?***

Ginger, was the forerunner and set the tone for her sisters by completing her program and graduating from high school. Aunt Nellie, encouraged her to "expand her horizons." Ginger boarded a bus for Los Angeles and began a new life. Her tie to home was Nellie's good friend, Mary. She rented a room in a house next door to Aunt Mary's, enrolled in several business courses, found a job, and began making friends. She eventually met a man, with whom, my mother said, she was well matched and married him and they had a good, though short life together. Circumstances of the war ended their relationship and Ginger was heartbroken.

After her high school graduation, Virgi moved into the apartment with Ginger and her husband and found a job at Woolworth's dime store. By the time Grayce arrived in LA, Virgi had moved out so Grayce moved in! Her first employment was at Woolworth's, in the job that Virgi had vacated.

Each of the girls married a man who had served in the armed forces during WWII, was a hard worker and a patriotic citizen. Each couple joined middle class America after the war: they purchased middle class homes, drove nice cars, paid their bills and their taxes. They all stayed in southern California, never living more than 65 miles apart. Their lives were entwined in a healthy way through all of their adult years. I believe their friendship and unbroken love for one another is what carried them through their griefs and their tomorrows. When I say 'unbroken', I mean, differences were settled, hurt feelings were mended, and apologies were given and received, even if some time lapsed. The blips were rectified. It was a mature love: each respected the other two. And each was committed to keeping their bond.

When I was born, April, 1945, World War II was winding down, my dad, George, was still overseas, and my mom and I lived with Aunt Ginger and her husband. A favorite story is that Aunt Virgi would come to the apartment every day and she and Ginger would dote on me, taking turns giving me a bath, dressing me, cuddling me, and then strolling me around the neighborhood in the perambulator. Two months after I was born Virgi's husband, an Air Force pilot, returned home from overseas just about the time his twin sons were born. My sisters, Marsha and Connie, were born within the next few years.

Ginger eventually remarried, a man named Phil, whose tank followed General George Patton during the Battle of the Bulge in WWII. They had a good life together until his death.

For the all their lives, Ginger, Virgi and Grayce kept in very close touch through letters, long distance phone calls, and visits several times a year. Their husbands got along well with each other, except when they didn't! But they always made up! My younger sisters and I remember those very frequent family get-togethers in the 1950's. The gatherings were most often at our house so that we kids would have our trikes and bikes and toys to occupy us, and also because our mom, Grayce, had the gift of hospitality and loved hosting the clan. Adult conversations around our dining room table were always energetic, filled with hilarious laughter. The men were often loud and boisterous and could be very argumentative. All six of the adults smoked and drank and participated in the fun. I remember lots of swearing by the men, in order to gain traction for whatever point they were trying to make. They talked about family issues, mutual friends, world events, politics, movies and movie stars. They reminisced about the War. They told jokes, played poker, and competed fiercely at a board game they called pooka. They barbequed hamburgers, hot dogs, or steaks, or feasted on Grayce's special enchiladas. We kids would hang over the dining room table, grab snacks, laugh at them laughing, and go back outside to play.

Time moves on -

Historians dubbed the 1940s the War Years, the 50s were the fabulous 50s. The 60s was often called the tumultuous decade.

In 1959, our family moved from H Street to M Street, five alphabet letters apart, but a distance of several miles across our small coastal town. My memories of the get-togethers on M Street are of more subdued gatherings. The group of six friends assembled as frequently, enjoyed each other as much. The 'smoking is dangerous' alert prompted the women to quit, with the men following more slowly. The drinking tapered off. They were all growing up. But also, society in the clamorous 60s had its own set of new and sometimes frightening challenges. It was a sobering era of cultural change.

During this time, Aunt Ginger became the personal secretary of one of the movie stars she had greatly admired in her childhood, and who is mentioned in her remembrances, Sue Carol. Sue had married the well know actor, Alan Ladd. As I remember, Ginger went to Sue's home twice or three times a week to answer Sue's correspondence, make appointments, go shopping, and be a friend. It was a long lasting relationship until Sue passed in 1982.

I'm remembering also that Ginger and Phil would hear by the grapevine that 'extras' were needed in 'crowd' scenes for movies that were being filmed in nearby Hollywood. Ginger and Phil would show up on the movie lot in case they could be used and hired for the day. They often were asked to arrive in clothing to fit the movie theme, such as the 1920s bootlegging era or western attire. I remember a really cute 'Roaring 20s' heavily fringed silvery dress that Ginger owned. Being an extra was just for fun, an opportunity to join the Hollywood hubbub and glitz. All the while they would be keeping their eyes opened for popular celebrities and listening for tidbits of interesting star gossip. Ginger enjoyed sharing stories of seeing several of the admired stars of the day.

Here are some fun photos of the Henry girls and two of the women who loved them and invested in them -

Ginger Henry at Big Bear Ski Resort, 1938

Ginger at the beach, 1939

Left to right,
Virgi, Grayce,
and Ginger, 1947

Left, Aunt Nellie, 1941
Right, Ginger and Aunt Harriet, 1945

The Ginger I knew -

Do you remember in her memoir that she determined to change her personality into becoming vivacious? She accomplished that. In her high school days she was popular, going on dates and enjoying Aunt Nellie's parties that gathered friends at their house to sing and laugh. I think of my aunt as very thoughtful, always studying how to answer, but also upbeat and outgoing in her own way.

My aunt was articulate and attractive, and quick to see the humor in every situation. She and her sisters loved to laugh! Contrary to her stubborn teenage decision to never let anyone cut her hair, she was always meticulously coifed and wore a beautiful, almost-shoulder length, champagne-colored bob. Her nails were her own, long and beautifully manicured and always polished, and her eyes were bright. She wore unique classy jewelry and simple, soft-colored, fashionable clothes …or kaftans with bright, artsy, splashes of color. She often brought my sisters and I small personal items on her frequent visits: a pen and a tablet, a piece of her jewelry, a souvenir from one of her travels. She was an excellent listener and was consistently interested in us girls and our lives. She had an air of refined grace and careful speaking, sounding like the intellectual she was. She continued to be an avid reader all her life.

Ginger was intrigued by other cultures and traveled to Thailand, the Philippines, and to Western Europe. She and her husband Phil invited my parents to go on vacations with them, but my daddy, George, was a homebody and my mom was not interested in going without him.

When my husband, and I became foster parents, my aunts were thrilled. Unfortunately my mom had already passed away. We have a really cute and funny picture of Aunt Ginger and Aunt Virgi with 6 year old David, the boy we adopted. He is clowning around and they are laughing uproariously. In her trust, Ginger designated a sizeable monetary gift to a local organization that worked with foster children. She did not forget her beginnings and gave back.

Ginger confided in me that she had never resolved the sadness of her early years, never really understood why their southern relatives had not sheltered the girls after their parents died. I believe each girl carried a sense of abandonment that they bravely overcame in their daily lives. After some years of corresponding with their aunts and uncles and cousins, and after long deliberation, the three sisters flew to Canton, North Carolina. I'm sure they had a tearful reunion and I know there was a reconciliation of relationships that brought them peace. They continued to correspond and exchange Christmas cards with several of them. Explanations were never made about the past rebuff, and because of the girls' good manners and propriety, the questions were never asked.

Ginger continued living in her beautiful suburban home after Phil died. Her gardener made sure her yard was always full of thriving greenery and lush with flowering plants. Over the years she had two uniquely gorgeous huge fluffy cats, Mashugana 1 and Mashugana 2. It is a Yiddish word that means nonsensical, silly, crazy. She loved their antics and they brought her and Uncle Phil a lot of joy.

My sisters, Marsha and Connie, and I, were the lucky recipients of Henry girls' affection and attention. Our mom and her sisters were determined to be consistently caring and upbeat women, in spite of their early years of destitution and distress. I know they experienced their seasons of grieving.

Ginger did not have children. Virgi and her husband, Cliff, had two boys who we have always thoroughly enjoyed being around. Unfortunately we have lost touch with our cousins.

Dan and I lived out-of-state but visited Aunt Ginger as often as we could. Connie and her husband, Jerry, also moved out of the area, and visited as often as they could. Marsha and her husband, Don, stayed in the Los Angeles area and devotedly visited her over the years. Marsha and Don were with Ginger, as was a hospice worker, when she passed away peacefully in her home in Thousand Oaks, California, in 2008.

Ginger was 92 when she passed. Virgi lived until her late 80's. My mom, Grayce, died at home where she was living with my dad, when she was 68.

Aunt Harriet (Eliza's sister)(also referred to as Aunt Hattie) and Aunt Nellie (the girls' exceptional foster mom) both lived in close proximity to our family while we were growing up. Aunt Harriet lived in a cute 1940's era stucco home about 20 miles away from our place. She was an amazing woman, a poet, a serious church-go'er. She would bake pies and forget the sugar, and cookies and forget the leaven. But she would laugh at herself and her sweet beautiful face would crinkle and wrinkle in the most charming places. Aunt Nellie moved to LA to live with Mary. She worked in Bullocks department store and gave us charming books for Christmases. I stayed with her a few times and on June 2, 1953, when I was 8, we watched

Queen Elizabeth's coronation on their tiny-screen black and white TV.

How I came to write *Remembering Genevieve -*

At some point in my early adulthood, Aunt Ginger mentioned that when she was in her twenties, she had written her childhood memories. Several times I expressed an avid interest in reading them. Eventually, I pressed her a bit, saying that I wanted to know more about my mom's early years and about their childhood. Because the three Henry girls rarely shared about their growing up years, my sisters and I were very curious about their lives.

Finally, Ginger said she would re-read the stories she had composed decades ago and mail them to me. By that time I had been living in another state for many years, and we only saw each other once a year.

Why did it take so long for her to get her memoir to us? I don't believe Aunt Ginger was reluctant to share her story with her nieces. I think she wanted to be sure that after she put in the effort of selecting the ones she wanted preserved we would still be interested. I also believe she knew that facing her past would be a challenging emotional journey for her. After her husband, Phil, died she had the time and energy for it.

Aunt Ginger was 82 years old in 2001 when she tackled the editing of her memoirs, removing scenarios which she felt were too private, too revealing, or uninteresting. The manuscript came to me, as I have replicated in this book, organized in the chronological order she had written it, and with paragraphs snipped out and the pages clipped together. I thought it was very spunky of her to take on the proofreading task. After she sent her memoir to me I made copies to share with Marsha and Connie.

This is the letter Ginger wrote when she sent me the folder containing her story:

September 30, 2001

Dearest Georgi -
I've spent a few months applying myself to culling a lot of excerpts from the material I wrote early in life about our childhood, as I promised to do. You might not find as much personal insight into your darling mother's reactions as you wish, but I naturally wasn't inside Grace's and Virgi's minds—I was probing my own mind and memories.
The 1940's dates that appear on the left sides of the pages are the dates that I sat down at the typewriter. Just think, I started the process when you were a year old! At that point, I was trying to free myself from an underlying homesickness I felt for the Smokey Mountains of Ellijay.
The transition from N.C. to Ventura, Ca., took place on a five-day train trip. We came directly to Uncle Lee's (Daddy's bro.) house and stayed while a tiny box of a house was being completed in a new development on Ventura Avenue.
Honey, I feel really burned out with this project. I think I should include Marsha & Connie in the notes' dispersal, but that would need to wait. Would you be willing to share it, however you choose, with them? If so, please explain that I have reached the saturation point with it.
Hope you're all well & zooming along!
My love to all,

Ginger

After I received Aunt Ginger's memoirs, I attempted to read them several times. But it was distressing to realize, and painful to grasp, that my adorable, warm-hearted aunts and my beloved mother, had suffered such challenges of poverty and loss. At each attempt I would lay the folder aside.

Growing up, my sisters and I knew that the girls' parents had died while they were children, that they had spent some time in foster care, that Aunt Nellie had been one of their foster moms, and that their relatives had not taken them in. But those days were not re-visited in any depth in our family get-togethers.

When I finally looked into the window of their past, I devoured their story. I had retired from fostering and my own life had settled, and I could face their past. Their story is plainly told, but heart-wrenching and poignant, as well as being a deeply transparent, self-revealing adult-unmasking of a distressing childhood.

The Henry girls had been deceased for a few years when I wrote my own memoir about our family's adoption and foster care experience, in 2015. At some point it occurred to me that my aunt's story could be an excellent follow up on the plight of the abandoned and needy children in our cities and the need for foster and adoptive homes.

About Ginger's manuscript –

I applaud my aunt for her perseverance in reviewing her memories, which she had written so many years before over a 14 month period. The dates (she mentions that they were in the upper corner of each page) range consecutively from March 26, 1946 to May 23, 1947, and the stories were written in six segments according to the cities in which the family lived, just as in this book. Once they moved to California they set their roots down deep.

There is no indication that Ginger made typed additions or corrections to her 1940's typed pages when she was reading them 54 years later. Both the font and the stroke of the typewriter keys are completely consistent throughout the original. In 1946 she had used a manual typewriter that I am sure she had passed on to the second hand store years before she did her proofing. As she reviewed her work, she did not re-write any of the scenarios, she simply eliminated stories that did not fit her parameters of personal disclosure by scissoring them away and tossing them out. Consequently, among the original paper-clipped 8 ½ " x 11" pages, there many stories on quarter and half sheets, and a few that are just 1 or 2 sentences, and therefore just narrow strips of paper.

The originals she passed to me in 2001 included a few penned explanatory comments: that the screened porch was recommended for tubercular patients, that Charles Lindbergh had flown solo across the ocean, that Frieda was a cousin. A few dates were added, and the name of a school remembered. And she added a handwritten tidbit about her movie star friend, Sue Carol. She was extremely proud and pleased to be Sue's personal secretary for over twenty years. I include the note here:

Isn't life full of bizarre quirks? My being a youthful fan of Sue's (Sue Carol) which later became a long personal relationship with her—35 years later in our lives.

It occurs to me that it was a kind and gracious gift from Above that the two women would become close friends. In her challenging childhood, a spark of pleasure for Genevieve was her movie star idols, whose pictures she taped on the walls of her bedroom. It must have been a boost to Ginger's adult self-esteem that she was treasured by a heroine of her youth and able to be useful to Sue in her correspondence and in companionship. I feel very thankful for that.

As an editor of Ginger's work -

In her writing, Ginger used quotation marks liberally. I kept the quotation marks to denote that a person was speaking or when what someone had said was being quoted; otherwise I used 'half quotation marks' in all of the other places that she wanted them.

I *italicized* the words that she <u>underlined</u>, kept all her spellings, and did not adjust grammatical constructions or tamper with her wording. It seemed arrogant for me to think I could polish certain things when the entirety carried such beauty. She was a gifted writer.

I did change some last names.

I also decided to eliminate three stories that involved men who inappropriately touched the girls. Two of the men were family friends and one was a workman building a house nearby. The girls did not appear to tell any adults of the incidents and Ginger reported them as a journalist would - they were just some more of the facts of their lives.

Initially, I intended to re-write and re-tell the childhood saga in the form of a juvenile historical fiction novel. But I quickly realized I could not improve upon Aunt Ginger's voice, her unique writing style, and the progression of her maturity in her vignettes.

I have not attempted to analyze my aunt. She would not have wanted that at all. I have not disclosed certain personal details that I am aware of because she would not have wanted that at all. This is not an expose.

This is an historical account of a segment of 'the old days' spoken through the voice of one who had lived it. I believe she would have been okay with it.

My goal -

One of my goals in my very short writing career has been to bring awareness to the continual need that exists for men and women of good character and loving hearts to become involved in foster care and adoption, never minimizing the challenges it brings to the host family to add other people's children to your own family, even temporarily.

With Aunt Ginger's memories, I had a provocative, well-told story from the foster child's point of view.

The child welfare system will never be perfect, because human beings are not perfect and life is not tamable (meaning: convenient or easy or able to be tamed). We can do the best we can to recruit and train the people who present themselves to foster and adopt our needy children, but we cannot predict the dynamics of the flow of the relationships and turns of events that are inevitable. Human beings are too complicated! And life is, and always will be, mercurial.

But we can continue to hire qualified and caring foster parents, and qualified and caring social workers to help orphaned, neglected and abused children to find a place of safety and a place of acceptance and love. We can hold everyone involved accountable to honesty and ethics.

Author's post script-

Having thought about and read their stories many times (my mother wrote her memoirs also), and entertaining deep compassion for each of the Henry girls because they carried a silent sorrow of personal rejection to their graves, it occurs to me: ***Hey! I would not be ME if the southern relatives had relocated the Henry girls and grafted them into their families in North Carolina!***

My beautiful mom would not have met my handsome soldier dad on the Greyhound bus on that lovely spring day in 1941!

What a lesson this story can be in 'moving on'— letting bygones be bygones – forgiving and forgetting.

Let's be grateful, let's count our blessings, let's not be fixated and become stuck on what we see as mistakes! The mistakes might be life changers, but they also just might be fortuitous, providential, divine. And they often work out for good. Even for very good.

Yes, process. Yes, get therapy. Yes, get medical advice. But, forgive deeply and make something beautiful of your life. With God, all things are possible.

Acknowledgments –

Many many thanks to my family and friends who were readers of my first-draft manuscript:

My husband of 43 years, Dan, writes books also, so we proof and edit and cheer for each other. Thank you so much for your commas and comments, and especially for helping me with formatting and computer issues. I love that you are a patient man.

My faithful returnees, all of whom have invested themselves in improving the lives of children. They kindly read my first book and consented to read for me again:

Kathryn Baughman, LCSW, CRC, retired, our son Tim's mother-in-law, a great encourager;

Jessica Lemaire, LCSW, our son Tim's amazing adventurous wife. They are foster and adoptive parents.

Alice Ledesma, LSW, very happily retired, who I worked under as a foster parent for 12 years;

and Bob and Janet Needham, RN, good friends for 40 years, who are also foster and adoptive parents.

With this book, also, you all were generous in your suggestions and supportive of my efforts.

Barbara Giles, who I met when we were in the second grade when we both lived on H Street, almost 70 years ago! You put on your editor cap and provided line-by-line proof-reading and contributed many constructive ideas. Balboa forever!!

Dr. Holt was my husband Dan's MFT supervisor, and friend, and his wife Judy is a former high school English teacher. Both of your specific advice and encouragement gave me the boost I needed at the time I needed it.

Special thanks to my Bethel bff, decaf latte friend, and most recent reader, Linda Johnson.

Thank you Cynthia Stipech, Linda Whitaker, Vera Bert, Judy Moss, and Angie Rosa, my faithful prayer partners. Ladies, you are gifts to me.

And with love and joy I have a special word for my sisters: Marsha and Connie, I love that we three agree that our childhood with our mom and dad, Grayce and George, and our aunts and uncles and cousins, was beyond excellent, even unique. We have recollections we will enjoy, laugh at, be-in-awe-of, embrace and cherish all our days. Just as Aunt Ginger and Aunt Virgi and our mom, overcame blips and snags in their relationships and kept their love for each other strong, so have we, so will we. I love my sisties.

- Dedication -

To Lewis and Eliza,
the grandparents I have not known
but expect to embrace
on that beautiful shore
in the sweet by and by ...

In the Sweet By and By
Joseph Philbrick Webster,
composer

Also by Georgann Lemaire:

What Then Will This Child Turn Out to Be?

An Introductory Handbook for
Foster Care and Adoption

With Articles by Dan Lemaire MFT
-Fetal Alcohol Syndrome-
-Attachment Theory-
-Adoption in the Bible-

This is a memoir of my husband's and my twelve years of fostering and adoption experience with stories, insights, and gleaned wisdom, as well as informative articles by Dan, who is a marriage and family therapist.

Made in the USA
Columbia, SC
08 October 2024

43937958R00080